GENTLEMEN

Somerset & Dorset Joint Railway

A VIEW FROM THE PAST

STEPHEN AUSTIN

Ian Allan

PUBLISHING

SOMERSET & DORSET JOINT RAILWAY: A View From The Past

Front cover: A down train passing Corfe Mullen Junction signalbox. It is not on the wrong line: the apparent double track is two single lines to Broadstone and Wimborne, and the train is heading for Broadstone. The year is 1913, by when the early coaches had been replaced by bogie stock and the Derby 4-4-0, of the type introduced in 1891, had been given a larger boiler to haul them.
From a painting by George Heiron based on a photograph from the Ian Allan collection

Front cover, inset: 'Somerset', over-romanticised by British Railways. *Reproduced by courtesy of the South Devon Railway Trust*

Back cover, top: Midford goods yard, viewed from the Long Arch Bridge. The yard has a weighbridge, shed and a 2-ton hand crane; access is controlled by a ground frame in the hut on the left. The greensward in the background is clearly a deer park, the grounds of Midford Castle. One of the through trains from the Midlands comes past during the last week of the service, September 1962. The train engine is BR Class 5 No 73049; the assisting engine is S&D 2-8-0 No 89 (now No 53809) (now preserved at the Midland Railway Centre).
W. Potter/Colour-Rail (SD148)

Back cover, bottom: LMS Class 2P 4-4-0 No 698 worked on the S&D for nearly 30 years, and is seen entering Broadstone station from the north with a down local service, the 5.10pm Templecombe-Bournemouth, in July 1959. The train is a Southern Railway 3-coach set built in about 1930.
G. H. Hunt/Colour-Rail (SD281)

First published 1999

ISBN 0 7110 2692 0

© Stephen Austin 1999

Published by Ian Allan Publishing

an imprint of Ian Allan Publishing Ltd, Terminal House, Shepperton, Surrey TW17 8AS.

Printed by Ian Allan Printing Ltd, Riverdene Business Park, Hersham, Surrey KT12 4RG.

Code: 9911/B1

Title page: A down Saturday extra, hauled by standard 4-4-0 No 635 and 0-6-0 No 60 (now No 4560), passes Midford on 31 May 1936. The back cover view at the same place shows how little this scene has changed over the years. *LGRP*

Below: Just round the corner from Chilcompton station lies the tunnel, barely more than a long bridge carrying a minor road from the village. When the line was doubled a second bore was put through beside the original one. Coming through the old bore is the down 'Pines Express' some time in 1938; engine is standard 4-4-0 No 698.
Real Photographs

Contents

Above: The Saturday afternoon excursion to Burnham continued to run until the end of the 1962 summer season, although after 1959 the S&D 0-6-0s were replaced by the GW equivalents. On 21 July 1962 No 2204 has run round after arrival. Both the passenger and goods sheds are still intact. Beyond are the Queen's Hotel and, behind the station, the Somerset & Dorset Hotel. (The signalbox on the platform is now in the Somerset & Dorset Railway Trust museum at Washford.) The photographer is standing on the excursion platform. *E. Wilmshurst*

Introduction

The bases of this book are the photographic collections of Col Rixon Bucknall and C. R. H. Simpson, which were bequeathed to Ian Allan Publishing Ltd. Some of the views have become well known, others less so, and we thought a selection in one cover might be handy for S&D lovers, or might be an appetiser to those who do not know the line. To broaden the picture, I have made a further selection from the work of the many photographers who have made their pictures available over the years.

The Somerset & Dorset Joint Railway is much admired, and rightly so. It stands as a superb example of enterprise, engineering and public service. Created by businessmen in the counties of Dorset and Somerset to meet the needs of its area, it steadfastly put those needs ahead of the pursuit of quick profit; which brought it to the brink of financial destruction. Through the unswerving loyalty and dedication of its personnel, it won through and gained the support of two great railway empires, but never lost its spirit or its dedication to its community. After more than a hundred years of service, an abrupt cessation of demand for its services caused the government, into whose management its very success had propelled it, to demolish it. That last event had nothing to do with the excellence of the railway and will not be referred to again in these pages.

The S&D is also the archetypal railway enthusiast's railway. On a single line of track, through picturesque stone-built stations, you could watch a train of two old coaches with a Victorian tank engine, a coal train, 12 corridor coaches hauled by two express engines, then a coach and a couple of milk tanks hauled by anything, one after the other, and all surrounded by farmland with not a satanic mill in sight. If you are a model builder, Bath was a terminal station with a grand roof and classical frontage but only two platforms, and, if anyone says you should not put an express passenger engine in a little two-track shed, you can — they did it in Bournemouth.

This volume is a run along the S&D, in distance from Bournemouth to Burnham, and in time from the 1860s to the 1960s. The line, its machinery and its scenery have been much photographed but mainly during the leisure boom in the 1960s, so here we have spread the picture to cover more of the whole. There is a concentration on the steam locomotive, which is common enough and cannot be helped — the

locomotive is after all the power source, the thing that can move, and the active element in any picture; on a line served by a more than usually distinctive succession of locomotives, it is bound to dominate the scenes.

Below: At midday on 30 June 1957, the signalman at Binegar station watches one of the Saturday extras pass. It is the 7.35am from Nottingham, 12 coaches hauled by a BR Class 5 and piloted over the Mendips by 0-6-0 No 44102. *G. F. Bannister*

Acknowledgements

I acknowledge the indispensable standard books on the S&D: both titled *The Somerset & Dorset Railway*, one by D. S. Barrie and C. R. Clinker and the other by Robin Atthill. A definitive map is published by Peter Kay, based on the Midland Railway's own maps. No general book gives adequate attention to recent history or to railways, but *Portrait of Somerset* by Bryan Little is better than most. I would also like to thank Mr M. Gates of the Somerset & Dorset Railway Trust for assistance, and Mr George Heiron for producing the original painting used for the cover.

The History of the S&D

A characteristic of the S&D was that it seemed to make a point of being old-fashioned. It usually (though not always) worked a step behind the rest of the world, which was one of the things that made it so endearing to its admirers and so repellent to its detractors. Its basic concept was outmoded when the railway was designed in the 1840s, being the linking of two seaports to bypass the expensive and hazardous sea passage round the British coast. That sounds a good idea when you put it in those terms, but in actuality there is little need for port-to-port transport as such. The ports are but stages in the carriage of goods to and from inland towns, whether for import or export or between traders within this island. Coastal shipping as a means of linking places within Britain declined as soon as railways were able to do the job, and many harbour facilities provided by early railway companies did not see as much use as anticipated.

In the case of the S&D the ports were Poole on the English Channel and Burnham on the Bristol Channel. The company saw itself as a sea-land-sea route from Europe to Wales and Ireland. When, in time, it realised that it was not going to make its fortune that way, it changed its main function to that of access to the rest of the railway network, shipping out the produce of the district and, increasingly, bringing in travellers from the industrial north to the sunny south.

Somerset

Here, as elsewhere, the railway promoters were the prominent citizens and business interests, and foremost among these was the Clark family. Cyrus Clark began a sheepskin processing business in Street in 1825. His brother James joined him and branched out into leather-working and then shoemaking. They were to the fore in the meetings, begun in 1850, to establish a railway linking Glastonbury with the Bristol & Exeter Railway at Highbridge — part of the effort to develop the Somerset

Moors, a marshy tract of land nowhere more than 20ft above sea level. It was to supersede the Glastonbury Canal, which had been opened in 1833 and was then owned by the BER. The Somerset Central Railway received its Act of Parliament on 17 June 1852 and was opened amid tremendous rejoicing on 17 August 1854. The engineer, Charles Hutton Gregory, had the usual difficulty of laying a firm road across the bogs and solved it by the usual means of binding the formation with bundles of timber faggots. The unfortunate canal, so recently a technological triumph, was thereupon closed down. The railway company immediately put in hand extensions at both ends, to Burnham and to Wells.

Dorset

At the same time another group of promoters was setting up a line from Wimborne, on the Southampton & Dorchester Railway (recently absorbed into the London & South Western Railway), to Blandford. The Dorset Central Railway received its Act on 29 July 1856 and was opened on 1 November 1860. Wimborne had no access to the sea but the LSWR, which ran the trains on the Dorset, worked them down to Hamworthy Junction and over the short branch to Hamworthy (then called Poole, there being no railway in Poole itself).

From the start the two companies intended to meet and amalgamate. Several directors sat on both boards and, perhaps more importantly, they shared the same Secretary. Robert Arthur Read came from the BER to join the Somerset Central in 1853 at the age of 23 and took the same post in the Dorset Central in 1854. He continued as Secretary of the combined company and then of the Managing Committee formed in 1876, and retired in 1891, having steered the railway through many a tribulation.

While the Dorset Central was building, the Somerset Central commenced an extension from Glastonbury to join the Wiltshire,

Somerset & Weymouth Railway at Bruton, the junction being near Cole. The Dorset Central was authorised to build a line from Blandford to Cole. In fact it built the northern part first and opened it from Cole to Templecombe on 3 February 1862, at the same time as the line opened to Cole from Glastonbury.

Although the two companies were born to marry, they were fundamentally incompatible. The Somerset Central was supported financially, and worked, by the Bristol & Exeter and was therefore broad gauge. The Dorset Central was worked by the LSWR and was narrow (later known as standard) gauge. Something, obviously, had to give, and the Somerset Central proposed to narrow its gauge when the BER working lease expired in 1861, buy its own rolling stock and run both lines itself. Independent in all matters, it bought a large parcel of land at Highbridge, there to build a new station and a workshop capable of undertaking all the maintenance such rolling stock would require. The BER took this pretty magnanimously, all things considered, even lending rolling stock for a period of five months

when, as you might expect, the Somerset's was not ready in time. The Great Western Railway, however, of which the BER and WSWR were but satellites, took a dim view of this narrow gauge line in what it regarded as its territory, and refused to co-operate with it at any time, then or in the future. That was why the Somerset Central made a priority of building the link to the narrow gauge Salisbury & Yeovil Railway at Templecombe and why the Cole-Bruton connection was never used. Narrow gauge working eventually began on 3 February 1862. Fortunately, the LSWR, which had absorbed the Salisbury & Yeovil, was as friendly as the GWR was hostile.

At this time the two companies agreed to amalgamate, which required another Act of Parliament, and the Somerset & Dorset Railway was legally born on 1 September 1862. The missing link from Templecombe to Blandford was completed under the new management.

Somerset & Dorset
As soon as Templecombe and Blandford were linked, the company was able to take over

Above left: The train which characterised the S&D from the 1920s to the 1960s was a rake of LMS coaches hauled by a 4-4-0 or an 0-6-0, or both. On 28 July 1951, a glorious summer Saturday finds 4-4-0 No 568 (now No 40568), built in 1928, and 0-6-0 No 59 (now No 44559), built in 1922, hauling the nine-coach 10am Bournemouth-Bradford past Wellow church. *G. J. Jefferson*

Above: An immaculate turn-out of both staff and rolling stock at Burnham on Sea in 1895. The Cudworth 2-4-0 is overspread by the coaches, except for the chimney which stands above them. *Bucknall Collection*

running the Blandford to Wimborne section from the LSWR. It also obtained running powers so that it could work its own trains from Wimborne to Hamworthy.

The coast-to-coast route was now complete but, sadly, it did not come up to expectations in the account books. The problem was not that the railway was not a success but rather the affliction that has crippled so many worthy people: debt. All the money coming in was swallowed by the banks in interest payments, leaving nothing to pay the operating bills, still less give a return to the shareholders. The purchase of rolling stock added to the burden — indeed, of six locomotives ordered from the Vulcan Foundry in 1866, only two were actually taken — potential traffic was lost, the company's maritime ventures were not profitable and it slid into bankruptcy. However, in those days the Government recognised that a railway exerted a profound influence on the trade and life of its district, and that, if an insolvent line was simply closed down, the resultant hardship could be a greater social liability than its debts. Therefore the Chancery Court took over direction of the company and ran it, through those ominously anonymous men the Official Receivers, from mid-1866 to 1870. During that period the trains continued to run, but under conditions of the most stringent austerity.

After this episode the company could have shrunk into itself, withdrawing services and laying off staff in a search for some inner fount of profit; instead, it looked outwards. The

commercial fields in which greener grass was espied included the great city of Bristol, the growing attraction of Bournemouth as a resort for the populace of the Midlands, and the Somerset Coalfield. The latter was served very comfortably by the Somerset Coal Canal, which extended from Dundas Wharf (near Conkwell) on the Kennet & Avon Canal, up the Cam Brook to Paulton. It had a branch up the Wellow Brook to Radstock, but that was not a waterway but a tramway.

Access to Bristol was blocked by the presence of the Bristol & North Somerset Railway and the BER Yatton-Wells branch. In any case, they were part of the broad gauge empire. But beyond Bristol was a narrow gauge company, the Midland, which was even then building a branch from its main line down to Bath. The S&D management lost no time in establishing friendly relations with the Midland and in planning a new line over the Mendip Hills to Bath. This was an enterprise of railway mountaineering most unusual for the south of England. True, steep gradients abounded on the existing line, but that was a matter of saving money on the earthworks and none of them was of significant length. Here, though, to cross the limestone massif involved an eight-mile climb from the Brue Valley, much of it on a

Above left: The first freight engines on the line were the John Fowler 0-6-0s bought in 1874 for the Bath extension, and one of these new machines appears in this group of the entire staff at Blandford. Also featured is motive power of a much older design — unless the horse counts as a member of the staff. *Bucknall Collection*

Left: The original station at Templecombe, serving as offices for the engine shed, the angular building behind it. On this May Day of 1958, the engines visible are S&D veterans. In the yard are 2-8-0 No 83 (now No 53803) and an unidentified Class 4F 0-6-0. The 4-4-0 No 563 (now No 40563) and 0-6-0 No 72 (now No 43216), with tender uncoupled, are standing on a siding on the site of the station platform. To their left is the original S&D line, now a siding, and left again is the LSWR Templecombe Junction line. On the far left a train with a Class 2MT 2-6-2T at the front has been stopped on its way back into the upper station. *P. H. Wells*

ruling gradient of 1 in 50, and a similar descent to Radstock. The gradient was only obtained by laying out an almost continuous sequence of curves all the way. The company bought up the Coal Canal tramway and used its course down to Midford, but, instead of following the canal round to Bath, it chose to make a short cut, over another fearful switchback, to come out into the south side of the city.

The extension was built well and built fast; ground was broken in the summer of 1872 and it was opened on 20 July 1874. One reason for the urgency was that the money ran out and the engineering contractors were only persuaded to carry on by the promise that they would be paid from the profits when trains were running. With the unerring judgement of hindsight, we can see how ironic it was that the Bristol & North Somerset was also in difficulties and was only completed to Radstock, as a narrow gauge line, after the S&D. Had the political wrangles taken a different turn, it could have been part of the greater S&D, whose trains would then have gone up through Pensford to terminate in Bristol. The history of the line, and indeed of the whole rail traffic from the Midlands to the South Coast, would then have been very different. One can visualise the streams of holiday expresses of the 1930s and 1950s stopping to change engines at Dr Day's Bridge Junction, or a 1990s 'Pines Express' dropping into Temple Meads, its driver changing ends of the high-speed multiple-unit and zooming out through Marsh Junction to head south for Bournemouth.

That reminds us that the trains did not yet go to Bournemouth but still used Hamworthy, fine as a port but not poised to expand — well, it couldn't, being surrounded by water. The LSWR projected a branch from Broadstone down the east side of Holes Bay into Poole, but it was the S&D which set up a wholly-owned company, the Poole & Bournemouth, to extend it to that fast-growing town. The partners cordially exchanged running powers and from 15 June 1874 both LSWR and S&D trains ran into Bournemouth (West).

The Bath and Bournemouth extensions transformed S&D operations. Henceforth the old main line from Evercreech Junction to Highbridge became 'the Branch', coal began to

flow from the collieries around Radstock, and, from the first day, two of the four daily passenger trains to and from Bath conveyed through coaches over the Midland to and from Birmingham. But the line was deficient in equipment and personnel and, once again, was carrying an insupportable burden of debt. Unable to satisfy its creditors, the Board decided to cast itself into the bosom of a richer company.

An obvious potential buyer was the Bristol & Exeter, which still held an interest. However, it was amalgamating with the Great Western, which hesitated and haggled exactly as it had done over the Bristol & Gloucester line 30 years before. At this juncture the General Manager of the LSWR, Archibald Scott, heard that the S&D was looking for a deal. It took him exactly eight days to contact James Allport of the Midland, inspect the line and its accounts, draw up a proposal for a joint lease, have it approved by both Boards and have it accepted by the S&D Board. On 20 August 1875 the lease was signed, to come into effect on 1 November; it was ratified by Parliament in an Act dated 13 July 1876. It is not the sort of thing that is recorded in official documents, but it must have happened that staff on the Midland, which was boldly blasting its way through the high Pennines to reach Carlisle, and on the LSWR,

Above: One of the very first batch of engines bought by the Somerset Central from George England in July 1861. This view of No 2 was taken after September 1862, when the S&D was formed. *LPC/Bucknall Collection*

Above right: The spacious station at Broadstone, looking south. This view was taken in the early British Railways years but the station was still equipped with LSWR signals, with their characteristic slender arms, modified in a curious way to bring them lower so they could be seen from beyond the bridge. In the platform is an 'M7' class engine on a Bournemouth-Brockenhurst via Ringwood service. *M. A. Arnold*

Right: A beautiful photograph of a down train passing Charlton on the Hill in about 1900. Four six-wheel coaches and two brakes are hauled by 4-4-0 No 15, the first engine of this type on the S&D. *LGRP*

which had already bought three railways to which it had no physical connection, were kindred spirits with the men who had equally boldly staked their futures on the push to Bath, and that no such spirit was to be found at Paddington.

The new leaseholders formed a Joint Committee to run the line and its Secretary

was, as we remarked, Robert Read. Without wishing to underestimate the labours of the men who kept the wheels turning, he was the hero behind the scenes who kept the railway together, and I can do no better than quote the description of him given by Robin Atthill: 'a man of vision, courage, vigour, integrity and utter devotion to duty'. Of such men were great railways like the Somerset & Dorset made.

Joint Railway

It is one of the well-known stories of railway history that only a month after the lease was ratified, the affairs of the railway were pitched on to the front pages of the newspapers by the pitch-in at Braysdown Colliery on 7 August 1876. The companies vehemently pointed out the investment they were putting into the line and that it had been run without serious accident hitherto; but the British Public finds nothing so much fun as slinging mud, especially at a victim in no position to sling any back. The S&D acquired a quite unmerited character of a ramshackle, lackadaisical concern, which persists to this day. 'Steady and

Above: Midsomer Norton station in the 1890s. A down stopping train hauled by one of the 0-4-4Ts is drawing in. The passengers, including a baby, waiting to join it are in their best clothes, possibly a wedding or some such party. Note the method of shifting a milk churn, by tilting it onto its edge and rolling it along. *Bucknall Collection*

Above right: Representing the company's waterborne stock, the *Alpha* was built in 1877. It was kept busy bringing rails across from Newport for the LSWR (thus avoiding having to pay the Great Western). Since the length of rails increased over the years, it twice had extra sections spliced into its hull to accommodate them. This view is at Highbridge Wharf, the scene of the flour incident, in 1924, the year before it was scrapped. A trainload of timber in LNWR wagons, not too well stacked and not lashed, stands on the wharf. *Bucknall Collection*

Dignified', perhaps, might suit one of the high-stepping Derby 4-4-0s lifting a maximum load up the long gradient, but the tag 'Slow and Dirty' is better reserved for the pantechnicons which nowadays to universal approbation pollute the Fosse Way.

The Joint Committee left the details of operation alone where these were found to be satisfactory (which gave the line a sense of continuity), but where action was needed they acted. A new Superintendent, R. A. Dykes, and Engineer, A. Colson, were appointed. The resources of the parent companies were brought to bear, broadly speaking the Midland taking care of what moved and the LSWR of what didn't. Permanent way and signalling were replaced with the latest equipment, including the new Tyer electric tablet system for single-line control which came out in 1878, new locomotives and wagons were supplied from Derby and operating methods were brought thoroughly up to date. On the other hand, Highbridge Works was re-equipped and continued to overhaul locomotives and build coaches and wagons, and those staff who could measure up to the new standards were encouraged; indeed, corporate spirit was boosted by the adoption in 1886 of a distinctive blue livery for passenger stock. The Somerset & Dorset Railway Company still existed but the Midland and LSWR bought all the shares and in 1891 appointed a Board of their own

directors, absorbing the administration into their own staff on Robert Read's retirement. The company was finally wound up by the Grouping Act of 1921.

The maritime interests touched upon above are outside the scope of this little album, but should be acknowledged as they were central to the original designs of the railway. The Guest family, ironmakers of Dowlais in South Wales, had a country seat near Wimborne and Sir Ivor Guest was on the Dorset Central Board. The railway financed wharfs on the River Brue in Highbridge and built a pier at the end of the Burnham extension. Passenger ships plied between there and Cardiff and the S&D created a subsidiary, the Burnham Tidal Harbour Co, to run its own shipping. But the Bristol Channel is a hazardous place — not for nothing were the toughest ships said to be built in 'Bristol fashion' — and even before the pier was finished the company was having trouble making and keeping a channel for ships to reach it. The Joint Committee made a determined effort to make the ferry service viable, buying a large ship, the *Sherbro*, in 1884, but gave it up in 1888. Freight services were

more successful; coal and railway rails were shipped in to Highbridge and produce was sent to Wales. It was busy until the depression of the 1930s, when the railway ceased running ships from Highbridge at the end of 1933. At the other end of the line, in 1866 the company began a service from Poole to Cherbourg using chartered steamers. However, it was not a

success and only ran for two summer seasons.

An addition to the system was made during the tenure of the Joint Committee. This was the Bridgwater Railway, incorporated in 1882 and opened on 21 July 1890. It was an independent company, but was leased to and worked by the S&D from the start. It was wound up in 1921. Bridgwater was a far bigger town than

Highbridge and fast trains were put on to Templecombe, enabling the LSWR to give it a London service in competition with the GWR. A smaller but more important addition was a cut-off from Corfe Mullen Junction to Broadstone, opened on 14 December 1885, which enabled trains to run through to Bournemouth or Poole without reversing. Other candidates for expansion were dropped, including one which was destined much later to be famous among a public with little interest and less knowledge in these matters. In 1893 the Somerset Coal Canal went bankrupt and offered to sell out to the S&D. The latter declining, the GWR bought it and converted it into a railway from Limpley Stoke to Camerton. This was the railway that, after closure in 1951, was hired to Ealing Film Studios for the making of its comedy *The Titfield Thunderbolt.*

Under Joint management the railway forged ahead. When the Bath extension opened the fastest passenger train from Bournemouth took 2hr 40min and the rest over 3hr. In the 1890s it was down to 2hr 10min and by 1904 one express did the run in 1hr 47min, the fastest schedule ever obtained. The range of services widened, and through coaches came down to Bournemouth from Nottingham, York, Newcastle, Leeds, Bradford, Manchester and Liverpool. The finest train was a restaurant car express direct between Manchester and Bournemouth introduced on 1 October 1910; this service received the title the 'Pines Express' when naming trains became the fashion in 1927. On the freight side, too, the partners made the fullest use of the line, most traffic being exchanged at Bath and Templecombe. An institution all its life was the night train from Bath, at times varying between 2.30 and 2.50am, to Bournemouth. Although classed as a freight, it carried anything, including passengers and mails, and was always known as the 'Mail'. Another important train was the 'Burton', the overnight express freight from and to

Birmingham Lawley Street, its main task being to convey a company train of beer through from the Bass brewery in Burton-on-Trent. To carry this tremendous increase in traffic, work was put in hand in 1884 to double the line; it was progressed desultorily, however, and in the end only 40 of the 102 route-miles of the whole S&D received double track. The main line was less busy south of Templecombe than north of it; the introduction of more powerful locomotives and a mechanical gadget developed by the Locomotive Superintendent, Alfred Whitaker, for exchanging tablets at speed rendered its continued working on a single track acceptable.

It is sometimes said that the Midland did badly by the S&D because it had a 'small engine policy'. There is no actual evidence that it had anything of the kind. Its engines were in the main no smaller than anyone else's, saving that small number of big and usually troublesome engines on other lines that grabbed a disproportionate share of the limelight. What it had was a traffic control policy and strict budgeting. It never spent money just to break some record and attract the attention of the press. If it was at fault at all, it was that its philosophy of fast, frequent, regular trains of set loads presumed an unrealistic degree of regularity and predictability in its customers. The comments on lack of motive power or the line being too expensive to work are just expressions of the universal railway conflict: the locomotive man blames the traffic man for springing unplanned demands on him, the traffic man blames the locomotive man for not having spare power units on the shelf, then they both turn round and blame the Engineer for not flattening the British landscape and controlling its weather. What is a valid argument is that Bournemouth was one of only three seaside resorts served directly by the Midland, the others being Southport and Morecambe, and the company was weak in coping with the particular demands of such resorts.

The story of the fortunes of the line from its zenith in 1914 is the all too familiar one, but it must be faced. The blithe assumption by the Government of the ordering of the railways on the commencement of war was followed in

1917 by a formal seizure of control which it never relinquished. Failure to make due recompense to the railways for services rendered was followed by the ineptly-structured Grouping. In the resultant *milieu* the two partners were put into the Southern and the London, Midland & Scottish Groups; the question of what to do with assets shared by companies which were now in different Groups — and the S&D was not the only example — was not answered (or, one suspects, even considered), so the Joint organisation was simply left as it was.

Having regard to the enormous disparity in the sizes of the Groups, it would have been far more rational to bring it wholly into the Southern. Had that been done (although here we are in the realm of speculation), subsequent events in the real world indicate that it might have fared a great deal better. It is evident in many walks of life that joint ownership, be the partners never so co-operative, is always at risk from the insidious thought, 'Am I investing more than my share of resources or labour into an enterprise from which the other party is

Above: A southbound freight under way, hauled by 0-6-0 No 60, built by Vulcan Foundry in 1890, with its second boiler, which dates this photograph after 1908. The train is passing Corfe Mullen Junction signalbox and level crossing, and taking the Wimborne line. The first wagon is an open with a tarpaulin lashed over its central bar, the second is an all-timber-bodied van. The driver takes advantage of the skimpy Midland-pattern cab to sit on the side-sheet to improve his view ahead. *LGRP/Bucknall Collection*

Above right: This train, in 1898, includes bogie coaches, six-wheelers and a through coach from the Midland, distinguished by its clerestory roof. The location is Mill Down, north of Blandford, where the railway and road are on the hillside above the River Stour. *LGRP*

making more profit?' This is not the first time it has been expressed in this context: the LMS thought it in 1929 and offered to buy out the Southern's interest, but the Southern was content with the situation and declined. One can say that this thought caused the S&D to be

pushed down the queue for investment. On the civil engineering side the Southern, collectively under the spell of Herbert Walker's electrification crusade, did nothing in the way of even minor improvements, while schemes for works which would have advanced services and saved running costs, such as a through line at Templecombe or a bypass to that ill-conceived entry to Bath, were invariably turned down. On the rails, it was over 15 years before the LMS got around to supplying any of the modern types of rolling stock. The LMS also had a civil engineering responsibility in the form of the line from Mangotsfield Junction to Bath, which was of inferior standard and was the weakest link in the whole north-south chain.

The excuse was, of course, the usual one of reduced margins. Another facet of Government policy was giving unemployed men in rural areas lorries and tarred roads and encouraging them to cream off business from the railways: an apposite metaphor where the S&D was concerned, as milk had always been one of its staples. The 1929 buyout was one of the

proposals from a committee set up in the LMS to investigate the line's costs and reduce them. It presented a package which, as packages are apt to do, contained some nasty surprises for the staff. The posts of Traffic, Locomotive and Engineering Superintendents were abolished; staff and rolling stock were removed from the remit of the Joint Committee and enrolled in the LMS; operationally the line was classed as a district, with a controller in the office at Bath. For its part, the Southern took the civil engineering into its Southampton district. Local facilities, including the Engineering office at Glastonbury and the entire works at Highbridge, were closed down. There were numerous redundancies — 300 at Highbridge alone, where just to rub it in the property was left as it stood, unused, until the white heat of Harold Wilson's technological revolution of the 1960s consumed it. These measures naturally gave a kick to the downward spiral of the rural economy and must have reflected in turn on the local traffic of the railway, but the owners had already decided that the value of the line was as a through route. The only positive

Above left: Highbridge Works, viewed from the footpath just below Highbridge Loco signalbox. On the left is the engine shed, then the water tower, smithy and offices. The biggest building is the engine repair shop. The engine on the right is on a turntable, surrounded by coal storage grounds. *IA Library*

Left: Blandford station at about the turn of the century. The signalman exchanges tablets with the fireman of a down train. The engine is No 35, one of the Neilson, Reid 0-6-0s of 1878. *LGRP*

Above: In about the year 1913, 4-4-0 No 68 pulls away from Bath station with a through train comprising the most modern and luxurious Midland coaches. The building behind the train is the entrance to a bonded warehouse, whose storage occupied the space beneath this end of the station. *Real Photographs*

developments were the building during the 1920s of some halts: Corfe Mullen, Stourpaine & Durweston, Charlton Marshall, Shoscombe & Single Hill and Bawdrip date from this period.

The cuts were implemented in the first six months of 1930, but emphasis on through traffic was pursued with less energy. Not until the days were lengthening in 1938 did the civil engineers complete an overhaul of the Bath branch and clear it for the locomotives of the Stanier regime. The first appearance of one on a revenue train was on 2 May 1938, when the down 'Pines Express' was hauled by Class 5MT No 5440. The 'Black Fives' were an instant success, lifting load capacity and slashing running costs and, had there been more of them to spare for this end of the empire, could have had a major impact on the working of the line.

One streamlining project which might have improved services from the local aspect was not carried through: a traffic pooling arrangement. In Bath, Radstock, Shepton Mallet, Bruton, Wells, Highbridge and Bridgwater, the S&D and GWR both maintained establishments which were close neighbours. The pooling proposal meant that, in each place, business would be taken by either company's staff and the receipts divided up later according to a formula; there would be only one set of books, and clerical work, cartage, etc, would be combined. Pooling worked perfectly well in many places between ostensibly rival concerns, but here the GWR replied that it did not anticipate the likely economies in working being sufficient to improve the net balances, which was a polite way of saying that it knew quite well that it was doing better than the S&D at those places and was being invited to subsidise it.

The GWR response was purely financial in tone and to that extent rational. It is also true, however, that the Groups were expected to work together where better service would result, and while separate commercial companies have to define their boundaries, the Transport Act of 1947 removed those boundaries in law and in fact. The S&D services were published in both the Southern and LMS timetables, but the GWR pretended they did not exist. The inexplicable thing is, though, that the same practice prevailed after Nationalisation when all the railways were supposed to be dedicated not to internecine strife but to the service of the nation. The treatment of the S&D is glibly explained as stemming from a dislike on the part of the Western Region management, inherited from the GWR and dating back to 1875, but that ignores the presence of overseeing authority in the form of the Railway Executive, the British Transport Commission, the Ministry of Transport and Parliament. The true mystery is not why railway staff kept up old animosities,

but why those bodies were so powerless, or disinterested, or both.

On 11 September 1939 all the through passenger services over the S&D were cancelled, largely because this and all other routes from the Midlands to the South Coast were expected to be fully occupied by military traffic. It soon transpired that the disruption of normal life by the exigencies of war was less than anticipated, and at the beginning of 1940 through coaches between Bournemouth and Bradford were reinstated. This was the start of a gradual climb back to the prewar range of services, although that was not fully attained until 1952.

In 1948 the line was placed in the Southern Region for commercial and civil engineering purposes but was operated by the London Midland Region. In 1950 the operating staff were Southern, the line and its traffic returns were in the Southern Region south of Cole and in the Western Region north thereof, while the rolling stock was still London Midland. Any unbiased observer would say

Above left: An unusual view of Midford Viaduct, taken in the summer of 1929, from the east side. Crossing under the third arch is the GWR Limpley Stoke-Camerton branch, which itself crosses over the Somerset Coal Canal and the road over the hill to Wellow. Prominent on the other side is the B3110 road, a new alignment built to ease the gradient up to Odd Down for motors. On the right are the little wooden station building, its signalbox and the Hope & Anchor Inn in front. *G. Wheeler*

Above: The double-track sections looked as a main line should. Here is the down 'Pines Express' of the 1930s, seven coaches hauled by LMS Class 2P No 630. The location is not specified, but is probably either Wyke Champflower or just south of Cole station. *Real Photographs*

that such an administration could not work, and it did not work, but the railway itself carried on working thanks to the strength of personality of its personnel. As far as they were concerned, regardless of the letters on the forms they had to complete, or the colour of paint being applied to which part of the fabric, they were still the Somerset & Dorset, and this was the finest period of their history in this regard: that they kept the railway together in the worst management chaos any railway has suffered.

This saga has a gloomy tinge to it, but it should not be taken that, out on the tracks, life was depressing. In the 1937 season, before it had the benefit of bigger engines, four through expresses each way travelled the line every weekday, 12 on Saturdays and usually, in the best S&D tradition, extras were put on at short notice. In 1947 there were but two on weekdays and six on Saturdays; in 1957 it was six on weekdays and 14 northbound and 18 southbound on Saturdays. Enginemen took a delight in raising the echoes from the mellow stone townships as they blazed away up the banks, making up time lost by inferior railways up north, passing stations kept spick and span by third- and fourth-generation S&D men whose pride in their calling never wavered.

S&D: The Constituents

Somerset Central Railway
Founded 1 December 1851, Act 17 June 1852, opened 28 August 1854 Highbridge-Glastonbury.
Extension to Burnham authorised 1855, opened 3 May 1858.
Extension to Wells authorised 1856, opened 3 March 1859.
Extension Glastonbury to Cole authorised 1856, opened 3 February 1862.

Dorset Central Railway
Founded 1854, Act 29 July 1856, opened 1 November 1860 Wimborne-Blandford.
Extension to Cole authorised 1857, opened Cole to Templecombe 3 February 1862.

Somerset & Dorset Railway
Founded by amalgamation 9 May 1862, Act 7 August 1862, took over old companies 1 September 1862.
Templecombe to Blandford (ex-Dorset Central) opened 31 August 1863.
Evercreech Junction to Bath Junction authorised 1871, opened 20 July 1874.

Templecombe Junction Railway (owner Salisbury & Yeovil)
Authorised 1866, opened Templecombe No 1 Junction to Templecombe No 3 Junction, with branch to Upper station, March 1870.

Wimborne-Hamworthy (owner London & South Western Railway)
Opened 1 June 1847, used by S&D trains from 31 August 1863.

Broadstone-Poole (owner LSWR)
Authorised 1866, opened 2 December 1872 and used by S&D trains from then.

Left: Mixed trains, common on the S&D in early years, survived on the Wells and Bridgwater branches until closure. Here a Midland 0-4-4T, with a coach and two vans, approaches Wells in the 1930s. The view is from the platform of Priory Road station; the GWR Tucker Street station is visible to the right of the 'trespassers' notice. On the far left is a water tank and the end of the S&D engine shed. *Real Photographs*

Above: This was a line where double-heading was an institution and you were guaranteed to see it each summer. This typical example from 1936 is the down 'Pines Express' entering Combe Down Tunnel, with LMS 4-4-0s Nos 697 and 634. *Real Photographs*

Poole & Bournemouth Railway
Proposed by Dorset Central 1859, Act 26 May 1865 as a quasi-independent company, opened 15 June 1874 Poole to Bournemouth West.

Bath Queen Square (owner Midland Railway)
Opened from Mangotsfield 4 August 1869, used by S&D trains from 20 July 1874.

Somerset & Dorset Joint Railway
Founded by Midland and London & South Western Railways 19 August 1875, Act 13 July 1876, took over old company 1 November 1875.
Corfe Mullen Junction to Broadstone authorised 1883, opened 14 December 1885.

Bridgwater Railway
Act 18 August 1882, opened 21 July 1890 Edington Junction to Bridgwater. Taken over by the LSWR on 1 January 1923.

S&D: Who Worked It

• Somerset Central lines worked by Bristol & Exeter Railway from 17 August 1854 to 28 August 1861, worked by itself to 1 September 1862, then worked by Somerset & Dorset Railway.

• Dorset Central Wimborne to Blandford line worked by LSWR from 1 November 1860 to 30 August 1863, then worked by Somerset & Dorset Railway.

• Dorset Central Cole to Templecombe line worked by Somerset Central Railway from 3 February 1862 to 1 September 1862, then worked by Somerset & Dorset Railway.

• Templecombe-Blandford and Bath Extension lines worked by Somerset & Dorset Railway from opening.

• All lines (including the Bridgwater Railway) worked jointly by Midland Railway and London & South Western Railway from 1 November 1875 to 30 June 1923.

• Worked jointly by London, Midland & Scottish Railway and Southern Railway from 1 July 1923 to 31 January 1948.

• Worked by British Railways Southern Region from 1 February 1948 to 31 January 1958.

• Worked by BR Western Region from 1 February 1958 until closure.

Left: A significant event in S&D history was the arrival of the Stanier Class 5MT 4-6-0. This is No 5432 making the first trial run on 29 March 1938, seen south of Midford. *LGRP*

Below left: The firm of Clark, Son & Co celebrated the centenary of the opening of the oldest part of the S&D, the Somerset Central, by chartering a train from Glastonbury to Burnham on 28 August 1954. Modest in scale, the excursion was run in style, with 0-6-0 No 64 (now No 43201) decorated — indeed, dressed overall — for the occasion and the patrons in party mood. *R. F. J. Told*

Above right: On August Bank Holiday Saturday 1954, Midland 4-4-0 No 40527 pilots No 34093 *Saunton* out of Bath on the 7.0am Sheffield-Bournemouth. *Rev A. G. Newman*

Right: At Evercreech Junction in the 1950s. No 40568 has been attached to the up 'Pines Express' (train engine Class 5 No 73052). They have to start away on a gradient of 1 in 195; the siding above is level. On the left two more 4-4-0s wait in the middle siding for trains needing pilots up the hill. *Real Photographs*

A Run Up the Line

On the Somerset & Dorset, as in most places, the railway builders were directed by the courses of rivers and followed, where applicable, the precedents set by the navigators of the previous generation. The original main line followed the River Brue inland to Glastonbury but then forsook it to turn round the north side of the Tor and follow the Whitelake River to Pylle. It descended to cross the Brue at Cole and then crossed the watershed near Wincanton. The rest of the route lay in the valley of the River Stour. The northern part of this is known as the Blackmore Vale, a huge, shallow but well-defined bowl with Templecombe in its centre. A 'gap' through Cranborne Chase brings us to Blandford and down to Wimborne. The Bath extension struck off over the Mendip Hills with little in the way of watercourses to help it, save a stream up to Prestleigh and the small River Somer from Chilcompton. At Radstock that joined the Wellow Brook, which the line followed down to Midford. Here the Cam Brook flowed in and the combined stream was renamed the Midford Brook — but at this point the railway curved away to burrow under Combe Down, to come out above Bath.

Bournemouth

At the West station, S&D trains shared the platforms with London expresses of the South Western, but they were regarded as the poor relations when by rights it should have been their own house. When the S&D first exercised running powers south of Wimborne, they went to Hamworthy, or Poole as it was then called to disguise its true whereabouts; then to Poole proper. Both were LSWR branches; the S&D was the instigator of the Poole & Bournemouth. The LSWR used it for mere portions of its trains, attaching them to the Weymouth expresses at Wimborne or, later, Bournemouth Central. With the growth of Bournemouth, the construction of the direct line from West to Central in 1888 and finally the completion of the Holes Bay curve on 1 June 1893, those portions became more important and the LSWR built a carriage depot on the down side. However, the hotel in Queens Road opposite the station was named the Midland Hotel and saw no reason to change.

A goods yard was provided but in summer was apt to be annexed by the passenger department, and most goods traffic used Poole and Hamworthy.

Outside the station a triangle was created when a curve across the top of the junction opened in 1893. (Branksome station was built at this time.) Inside it were a coal yard and the S&D locomotive depot, called Branksome. The latter was used only for turn-round servicing, run as an out-station of the main depot at Wimborne until 1925, then of Templecombe. It had a turntable and coal stage (though they were disused by about 1934), and a small engine shed. Oddly, it had an establishment of enginemen but no artisans or locomotives.

Above left: For most of the life of the S&D, journeys began at Bournemouth West. Here an immaculately turned-out train is making ready to start. The engine is No 18, one of the first 4-4-0s supplied by Derby Works in 1891, and the photograph was probably taken soon after delivery. The first coach is a Highbridge-built six-wheeled brake. A man, blurred because of the length of the exposure, is on the side of the second coach, probably cleaning; his bucket is nearby. *Bucknall Collection*

Left: A down train descending the 1 in 60 incline from Parkstone to Poole. It comprises six six-wheeled coaches drawn by 4-4-0 No 15. The engine is carrying a boiler fitted in 1905, which has different chimney, dome and safety valves from the type shown in the previous view. *Locomotive Publishing Co*

Above: Near the end of their run, down S&D trains ran through the Bournemouth built-up area in what became the up direction when the Poole & Bournemouth became part of the main line. Looking west from the road outside Branksome station on 21 May 1954, 2-8-0 No 83 (now No 53803) brings in an LMS corridor third, two brake composites and a GWR full brake (probably for milk). These freight engines were often used on stopping passenger trains to fill in their duties. *H. Gordon Tidey*

Below left: Trains stopping at Broadstone were turned into the loop platforms; for one thing, they were nearer the entrance. This is a down S&D train, engine Neilson Reid 0-6-0 No 72. The structure in the right foreground is a signal post and the white sticks are attached to its guy-lines to make them more visible. *LGRP*

Above right: At Shillingstone station in the 1890s. A 4-4-0 engine runs into the platform and the signalman exchanges tablets with the fireman. *LGRP*

Centre right: Spetisbury station, seen from the vantage point of the prehistoric fort known as Crawford Castle. It was not provided with a passing loop and was not a true block station, but the disc and crossbar signal was kept in use for indicating whether there was custom for trains booked to stop on request only. It was abolished on 16 April 1901 when double-track working began on this section of the line. *LPC*

Below right: Just south of Templecombe, where the line crosses under the main A30 road. The train is the down 'Pines Express', hauled by Class 5MT No 44839, in August 1950. The coaches, all LMS standards, are alternately in LMS and BR liveries; could a shunter with a sense of humour have arranged them? *Real Photographs*

Broadstone

The Poole branch lay alongside the original Southampton & Dorchester main line for half a mile up to the station in the heathland village. The junction was at the north end of the station, where the direct curve from Corfe Mullen also fetched up. This was the southern end of the S&D itself.

Corfe Mullen Junction

The new curve left the original line here but stayed alongside it as far as the next level crossing, then gradually diverged and climbed away to a summit in the Corfe Hills. Then it dropped down to Broadstone. When the old line was finally removed in 1933, a mile was retained from the junction to Carter's clay pit.

Wimborne

The most important town in this corner of Dorset when the Southampton & Dorchester Railway was built (Bournemouth did not then exist) was a major junction. A marshalling yard, engine shed, turntable and staff housing were built at the S&D junction, which lay south of

the river near the hamlet of Oakley. Passenger trains were withdrawn in July 1920 and freight trains in February 1932.

Bailey Gate

This was the name given to the station in Sturminster Marshall. When the Corfe Mullen cut-off was built it began here but was laid alongside the old line as far as Corfe Mullen, giving the impression of a double track. A large milk depot was built here by Dorset Modern Dairies Ltd, a firm later absorbed by Wiltshire United Dairies.

Spetisbury (Spettisbury on older maps)

This was a minor roadside village on the Stour. The station lay beside an Iron Age hill-fort known as Spettisbury Rings or Crawford Castle, the line cutting through the outer earthworks. Here in AD43 the Second Roman Legion attacked and captured the fort, and the story is that the railway navvies unearthed a quantity of human remains from that battle.

Blandford

Blandford has a collection of Georgian town

Above left: Another view of the 'Pines Express', showing the whole train of 11 coaches. The engine, No 44830, which was based in Bristol for many years, has received a BR number, but the rest of the train is in LMS colours, for this is the summer of 1949. It is on the double-track section north of Templecombe, coasting down towards No 2 Junction. *Real Photographs*

Above: On the Templecombe Junction Railway; and another era of motive power, on Saturday 1 July 1961. The train is descending from No 2 Junction, in the background, past the yard tracks which lie on the site of the original S&D line. Going off to the left is the link line to Templecombe SR. The train is the 10.20am Liverpool-Bournemouth (which on Mondays to Fridays was part of the 'Pines Express') hauled by BR '4' 4-6-0 No 75027 (now preserved on the Bluebell Railway) and 'West Country' No 34039 *Boscastle* (now preserved on the Great Central Railway). Standing on the ashpit is No 40634, a standard Derby 4-4-0 which was sent new to the S&D as No 45 in 1928. *J. C. Haydon*

centre buildings unsurpassed in England, the result of a more than ordinarily destructive fire in 1731. It was rebuilt under the direction of two local architects, John and William Bastard. The Dorset Central terminated in the adjoining hamlet of Blandford St Mary, on the south side of the river, until a bridge over the Stour was completed. The town grew to the east of the railway, the west side being bounded by the grounds of Bryanston House, known since 1927 as a public school.

Blandford Camp, on the hill east of the town, was served by a three-mile branch, which left the main line just north of the river bridge and operated intermittently from 1918 to 1928.

Stourpaine

Better known in recent years for the 'Great Working of Steam', Stourpaine adjoins a huge Iron Age hill-fort on Hod Hill. This, like Crawford Castle, was captured by the Romans and used by them as a camp. The halt serving Stourpaine and Durweston was a platform on the single line: in 1901 a loop was built half a mile further up, immediately south of Hodmoor Bridge over the River Stour. After World War 1 it was used only occasionally, the signalbox being otherwise switched out, and it was reduced to a ground frame in 1925.

Shillingstone

The village looks across to yet another hill-fort, Hambledon, which was in military use as recently as 1759 when General Wolfe used it to rehearse his attack on Quebec. It was formerly Shilling Okeford. Here the line emerges into the broad bowl of the Blackmore Vale.

Sturminster Newton

This is the new town formed after the 16th century bridge was built across from the Stour Minster.

Stalbridge

The 3½ miles from Stalbridge to Templecombe contained an unusually large number of level crossings, seven. In the middle of it was Henstridge, a full station but with no loop and only a single siding. The boundary from Dorset into Somerset was crossed three-quarters of a mile north of Stalbridge station.

Templecombe

The S&D was dependent for its operations on using a piece of railway that did not belong to it. In 1862 it had a terminal station on the north side of the Salisbury & Yeovil line — in the following year it was extended southwards under the latter — and from the yard a curve ascended to join the S&Y to the east. In order to exchange traffic, trains had to ascend this curve and reverse down the main line. To improve this the S&Y built the Templecombe Junction Railway, which left the S&D at a point called Templecombe No 3 Junction and rose alongside it to No 2 Junction.

Above left: Cole station lay in a picturesque setting between the village and the River Brue. On Saturday 24 August 1957 the 2.20pm Highbridge-Templecombe, one of the five daily branch services, heads south. 0-6-0 No 62 (now No 43194) was one of the longest-lived engines, built in 1896 and scrapped in 1960. *R. Downes*

Left: The 2.20pm Highbridge-Templecombe, with engine No 73 (now No 43218), stands in Evercreech Junction station, not needing the water column which replenished many a tender emptied by the slog over the Mendips. Beyond the level crossing, the line falls to the River Alham and rises beyond towards Lamyatt Crossing. *R. E. Toop*

Here a branch curved round to the west to reach the S&Y station. The line continued down to rejoin the S&D at No 1 Junction, under the road bridge by the station. This line, opened in March 1870, was leased to the S&D, which paid a rental to the S&Y, later the LSWR and then the Southern Railway, although after 1922 it was a paper transaction only.

In 1887 the original station, bypassed, was absorbed by the locomotive depot, which became more important when Wimborne was closed, and received a new engine shed as late as 1950. No 1 Junction was removed and a rudimentary platform, named Templecombe Lower, was erected under the railway bridge. An occasional train used it, just for a change, but most used the Upper station. Up trains had to back into it to make the call and down trains had to back out to resume their journey, the reverse movements being made by attaching an engine at the rear to pull back. Only one platform was provided in the Upper station; a common movement was for a terminating train from one direction to pull in, unload, then move out to stand on the double track between the station and No 2 Junction, while another train from the other direction came up past it. No passenger trains ran through between north and southwest, except between the wars, when there was an irregular summer holiday service from Derby to Sidmouth and Exmouth.

Wincanton

This was the location of milk processing factories set up by Dried Milk Products Ltd and Cow & Gate Ltd.

Cole

The original connection to the Wilts, Somerset & Weymouth line diverged on the up side just north of the crossing. It was lifted when the gauge was narrowed in 1863 and never reinstated. A station with a small goods yard was placed here, intended to serve the town of Bruton, a place where nothing appears to have stirred since the dissolution of the monastery.

Evercreech Junction

The junction, where the Bath extension curved off to the right and immediately began its ascent into the Mendip Hills, lay a quarter-mile

Left: At Evercreech Junction itself, a signalman's view of a down freight, mostly coal, hauled by LMS Class 4F No 44235, coming round the curve of the Bath extension to join the original main line. Most freights stopped here for examination and an engine change; in the fork of the junction off to the left is a turntable and in view is a pit for cleaning fires before the return working. The date is 1 June 1951. *T. J. Saunders*

Below left: A coal train from Norton Hill Colliery on Charlton Road Viaduct, approaching Shepton Mallet, on the morning of 17 July 1953. The engine is 2-8-0 No 87 (now No 53807). *D. T. Flook*

Above right: Passing Masbury halt, LMS standard 4-4-0 No 40563, based at Templecombe for many years, pilots 'West Country' No 34044 *Woolacombe* on the up 'Pines Express' in the mid-1950s. One wonders what exigency forced them to add that ancient S&D coach to this important train. It also looks as though *Woolacombe* is not doing too well, as the fireman has in his hand a fire-iron which he is unwisely allowing to project outside the cab. *Real Photographs*

Centre right: The summit in Masbury Cutting. Standard 4-4-0 No 630 has lifted the winter formation of the down 'Pines Express' without difficulty and even has surplus steam. *Real Photographs*

Below right: Passing Norton Down in a stopping train (the 9.5am Templecombe-Bath), we meet 2-8-0 No 89 (now No 53809) climbing the hill with a freight. The date is 24 March 1960. *E. W. J. Crawforth*

beyond the station. Taking advantage of the generous broad gauge layout, a siding was placed between the up and down platform lines, used for terminating branch trains and for banking engines to stand by between assisting duties. As the Bath line passed right by the village of Evercreech, a new station, Evercreech New, was provided there.

Pylle

The station's claim to fame is that it was by the Fosse Way, which in that part was still a main highway (and became a motor road, MoT A37). The S&D intersected that ancient road again: between Shepton Mallet and Cannard's Grave crossroads (Fosse Lane Bridge); near the North Somerset viaduct, Radstock; and above Devonshire Tunnel.

Glastonbury

This was in the 1850s the only sizeable town in the area. In ancient times, as you came eastwards, this was the first permanently dry ground you reached, hence its strategic importance and its eighth century Abbey.

It was the junction for the Wells branch, which extended alongside the main line for a

Above: Radstock station from the footbridge. Behind it are the buildings of Coombs' Brewery, one bearing the date 1898. The main road crosses the railway at the far end of the forecourt. The train, hauled by an 0-4-4T, includes two of the elliptical-roofed coaches introduced in 1898. *Bucknall Collection*

Above right: A view eastwards from Radstock station shows the goods facilities and beyond them the engine shed. Behind the shed a branch goes off to the right to Ludlows Colliery. *LGRP*

mile, resembling a double track. Adjoining the station was a house, 'The Pollards', the headquarters of the line until the move to Bath in 1877 and subsequently the Engineer's office. In the yard were private sidings for Snow & Co, timber merchants, Garvin & Co Ltd, Avalon Orchards Ltd, The Near Honey Co Ltd and Torvex Peat Co Ltd, a list which sums up the industries of the area. A famous son of the town was John Morland, who in 1870 began making sheepskin products. The neighbouring town of Street was the headquarters of C. & J. Clark, which employed over 5,000 people around Somerset and became Britain's largest shoemakers.

Wells

This cathedral city, which owing to its small size was much inclined to stand on its dignity (in an attempt to look taller) was blessed with three stations: the Somerset Central's Priory Road of 1859, the East Somerset's of 1862 and the Bristol & Exeter's Tucker Street of 1870. The first two were end-to-end, separated only by the street Priory Road. When the last was opened, the B&E and ES expressed a wish to join up, but that could only be done by going through Priory Road and putting a track across the goods yard at almost a right angle, complexity being compounded by the fact that the S&D had just converted to narrow gauge while the other two were still broad. The Board of Trade Railway Inspector forbade its general use on the grounds that insufficient safeguards existed for trains cutting across the S&D shunting lines. When the B&E and ES were converted to narrow gauge in 1878, passenger trains began using the link and the East Somerset station was closed. Great Western Yatton-Witham trains had to use nine chains of S&D property.

Snow's had a rail-served timber yard and the East Somerset and S&D both had small engine sheds.

Highbridge

Highbridge, the first connection with the rest of the railways and the point where construction started, was a port and industrial town on the River Brue where it entered the estuary of the Parrett. The Somerset Central terminus was alongside, and joined to, the Bristol & Exeter station. At the north end the line crossed the B&E on the level to reach the goods yard, cattle market, wharf and Bland's timber yard, and the Burnham extension branched off at the goods station.

The company had the foresight to buy a piece of land on the north bank of the River Brue, and here in 1862 it put up its first repair shop for the rolling stock then being delivered so that it could run its own services. The Works eventually employed over 300 men and included a locomotive repair shop, carriage and wagon building and repair shops, boiler repair shop, foundry, smithy, sawmill and a locomotive running depot. The high qualities of performance, reliability and safety which characterised the railway's equipment were due to its possession of this excellent facility.

The connection between the two routes at the flat crossing did not see regular trains, but the GWR ran holiday excursions to Wells and Bournemouth, and the S&D similarly ran to Weston-Super-Mare.

Burnham

As a port or resort, Burnham was a forlorn hope. Beyond the little station, the rails extended down a slope of 1 in 23, on to a jetty which projected to reach what was, at low tide, a narrow channel with open water over four miles away. A large 'excursion' platform was provided to cope with the crowds of revellers, and the brick-making firm Colthurst, Symons & Co had a siding.

Edington Junction

This lay in the heart of the peat-bogs near the supremely optimistic Burtle Hill, an eminence rising just 10ft to an altitude of 23ft above sea level.

Bridgwater

Also a port, further up the Parrett (which was navigable up to Ilchester), Bridgwater was the terminus of the Bridgwater & Taunton Canal and was a much bigger and more important place than Highbridge. The Bridgwater Railway terminated midway between the town and the GWR station, and had a half-mile branch to a wharf of its own on the river and a siding serving Barham's brickworks. As the GWR branch to the docks ran past the station's front door, a connection was made to maintain access to the wharf after the branch was closed in 1954.

Shepton Mallet

A prosperous wool town in olden times, its mills were driven by the Doulting Water, but then it stagnated until the railway was projected. In 1860 Francis Showering set up the Kilver Street Brewery, which in the 1950s became famous through its product named 'Babycham'. Clark's also operated here and was the biggest employer.

Charlton Road station was the site of the railway's ballast plant and the Signal & Telegraph depot. To the north were the S&D's longest viaduct, Charlton Road (317yd), and its highest, Bath Road (62ft). The latter gave everyone a fright but luckily nothing worse on 2 February 1946; it was one of those widened

when the line was doubled, and the engineers had removed the track and decking of the new part for inspection when the middle arch collapsed. It took six months to rebuild it, and of course it cast doubt on the quality of work on the other duplicated viaducts, so they were all given an overhaul.

Winsor Hill

At the north end of the short tunnel stood a signalbox controlling two systems of sidings serving nearby quarries; Hamwood on the down side and Beachamp's on the up side.

Masbury

The summit of the line, 811ft above sea level; exposed to the wet west winds which come in from the Bristol Channel and regularly bring snow. Masbury Castle is another hill-fort, the depiction of a stone tower on the frontage of the station house being entirely imaginary. The station was reduced to halt status in 1935.

Binegar

The station had sidings for two more quarry companies, Read & Son and Dalley's. After the Depression these firms folded, as did many others, and were taken over by a national conglomerate, Roads Reconstruction (1934) Ltd. Into the goods yard came a private 2ft 6in gauge railway from the Oakhill Brewery, 2½ miles away, which had a short life, opened in 1904 but demolished in 1921.

Morewood Sidings

A mile down the line from Chilcompton, this was an important centre serving the Emborough Quarry, and was linked to Cockhill Quarry by a cableway and to Morewood Colliery by a 2ft gauge railway.

Chilcompton

This was another place with a prestigious public school, Downside. It was the loading point for New Rock Colliery, which lay a mile to the south and was unusual in having no rail connection.

Midsomer Norton

The very name is redolent of bees among flowers in a sunny, sleepy garden — and that

Above: This close-up of Radstock engine shed, during the period when the Somerset & Dorset Railway Trust was in occupation, also reminds us of the Mendip winter, when snow clogs up outdoor machinery and ice makes every step a hazard. *Author's Collection*

was exactly the image of the station. It regularly won station garden awards from 1913 until closure. Beyond its fence, however, the place was just a dreary mining town. Norton Hill Colliery, on the down side north of the station, was the largest in the area and employed two locomotives on its internal railway.

Radstock
This was the centre of the Somerset Coalfield, where the first coal was raised in 1763, and by 1900 some 6,000 men worked in the pits. The collieries of Clandown, Middle Pit, Ludlows, Tyning, Upper and Lower Writhlington, Foxcote and Braysdown were served by the S&D, while Old Welton, Ludlows, Kilmersdon

and Huish were connected to the GWR. The branch line to Clandown dated from the opening of the Somerset Coal Canal, of which it was a feeder. These mines had both standard gauge sidings and narrow gauge internal tramways.

The British Wagon Co, later Wagon Repairs Ltd, had a depot, and sidings served the gasworks and the Radstock Co-operative Society bakery. To the east of the station, on the down side, was a small two-road engine shed, a most attractive stone building. It housed the engines used for shunting in the area. A branch curved away on the far side of the shed to Ludlows Colliery, through whose yard it was possible to reach the GW line. Other than that there was no connection, although the two stations were side by side and the lines crossed a few yards to the west.

Wellow
Onwards from Radstock and through Wellow the line was a straightened-out version of the Somerset Coal Canal Tramway, and fragments

Left: Kilmersdon Colliery was not, strictly speaking, on the S&D as its rail connection was to the Great Western line south of Radstock station, but these views, taken in 1967, are typical of the arrangement for taking coal out of the mines. This is the loading plant, with a narrow-gauge skip wagon on the gantry over standard-gauge wagons. The white crosses on the latter mean that they are not to go outside the NCB yard. Coal is shipped out in the BR steel wagons behind them. *C. J. Peacock*

of the engineering works of both the latter and the never-completed waterway remained along the route.

Midford

This might have been designed with the railway modeller in mind. Descending at 1 in 60, you passed a small goods yard, on the site of the transhipment wharf from the tramway to the Somerset Coal Canal, and came out on the 180yd viaduct. In the middle of this the double track became single. Its eight arches spanned a road, the Cam Brook, the Canal and the GWR branch line. (This was the location for the opening scene of the feature film *The Titfield Thunderbolt*.) At the far end a narrow platform with a small wooden building was perched on a steep hillside. Then there was another minute goods yard with two sidings, whence the line climbed at 1 in 50, round the hill on which stood Midford Castle, towards Combe Down.

Bath

The station was called, by the Midland and the S&D, Queen Square. Not that it was in Queen Square: that was where the company's head office was after 1877, a respectable address where one of the first residents was the Prince

of Wales. The station was on the corner of Seymour Street and James Street, so the people naturally called it Green Park. It was referred to as such in Ward Lock's *Shilling Guide*, which noted that it was 'one of the largest in the West of England and its façade is of elegant design'.

After Grouping it was Bath (LMS), as distinct from Bath (GWR). British Railways adopted Green Park, naming the GWR station Bath Spa. It has been said that the station was over-elaborate as a terminus for the branch from Mangotsfield, opened in 1869, but that ignores the status of Bath as a resort. The mineral springs were made the focus of a purpose-built holiday town by the Romans, and its pre-eminence as a genteel resort for the fashionable was established from the beginning of the 18th century through the efforts of Richard Nash. The waters were officially stated to be beneficial to cases of 'gout, rheumatism, neuralgia, sciatica, lumbago, paralysis, nervous debility, feminine ailments, digestive disorders, albuminuria, tropical anaemia, metallic poisoning, eczema, lepra, psoriasis, skin diseases, joint diseases and weakness, and throat diseases'. The Midland Railway was obviously bound to provide a commensurate station. We may also assume that it was built with the S&D

Above: The pithead buildings from the other side. Mr M. L. Parfitt of Radstock is loading coal from a wagon, for local sale. Moving into the sidings is the colliery's own engine, Peckett No 1788, delivered new in 1929 and retired in 1974 when the mine closed, and now preserved by the Somerset & Dorset Railway Trust. *P. J. Fowler*

Right: On the way from the main line to the colliery, No 1788 stops a safe distance from the Radstock-Kilmersdon road as its fireman alights to open the crossing gate. These views were taken on 11 August 1970, by which time this was the last Somerset mine in operation. *P. J. Fowler*

extension in mind, for the latter was announced as soon as the branch opened.

The passenger station was bounded at the platform ends by the River Avon. This limited the platform length to nine coaches of LMS stock, so in later years, when a 12-coach train of BR stock with two engines came in, the rear five coaches were off the end over the bridge. On the west side of the river lay the goods yard, south of the line, and locomotive depot, north of it. The latter was hemmed in by a branch line curving down to riverside wharves and Bladwell's timberyard. Beyond this lay the Victoria Works, home of Bath's most famous industrial concern, the crane manufacturers Stothert & Pitt. Further west, the gasworks sidings lay on the north side and the S&D diverged to the south. It turned through nearly 180° and climbed at a gradient of 1 in 50 to the tunnel under Combe Down. Half a mile up this fearsome bank were two private sidings, May's (Victoria Brick & Tile Co) and the Bath Co-operative Society's. Working them was a matter of more than ordinary difficulty. Wagons were taken up by the freight train banking engine, which pushed them up on the rear of the train being banked and then came down with them, so that the engine was on the downhill end of the wagons. No more than nine wagons could be left on the main line, and if there were more than four they had to be taken up by a separate trip and have a 20-ton brake van attached at the south end.

Right: The incline top, with a handbrake for the cable and a movable scotch to prevent an empty wagon from running back down. The winding house contains no motive power, gravity being the only propulsion. *C. J. Peacock*

Centre right: In October 1965, the incline brakesman begins to let a loaded wagon down. In the foreground the up-line cable is taut as it hauls in an empty wagon. Despite the apparently vulnerable situations of the staff, incline operations were safe and reliable. *C. J. Peacock*

Below right: Lower Writhlington Colliery, a mile east of Radstock station. The shaft winding frame stands above a loading shed, served by a single siding. The track to the right leads on to Foxcote and Upper Writhlington Collieries. To the left are a workshop and a drainage pump housed in a typical beam engine house. The S&D main line passes in front, and the signalbox, Writhlington, is the descendant of a cabin named Foxcote, erected here on the opening of the line and used as an intermediate block post — illegal, as the line was then single. The wagons are from Braysdown, a colliery up on the hill behind the camera. At their head is No 25A, one of the three little engines built by Highbridge Works for shunting the Radstock area.
Bucknall Collection

Left: Leaving the mining area, we head towards the hills blocking our way to Bath. On this day, 24 March 1960, the train approaching is hauled by one of the final additions to S&D motive power, BR Class 4 4-6-0 No 75071.
E. W. J. Crawforth

Below left: The line from Radstock to Midford, though basically direct, curves continuously. Just south of Midford station the down 'Pines Express' runs above the Wellow Brook, opposite Midford Hill, in 1938. The engine is No 698.
Real Photographs

Above: At Midford the double line from Templecombe becomes single. The junction is on the viaduct, on the left of this view. Goods facilities are dispersed; one yard is below the camera — the turnout in the foreground is its entrance — and the other on the far side of the valley. The passenger station is in a cramped site at the far end of the viaduct. The train, the down 'Pines Express' of 14 June 1952, comprises 10 coaches hauled by Class 5MT No 44839. The first and fourth coaches are timber-bodied, dating from 1925-1928, the others are later steel-clad stock. On the skyline above the second coach is Midford Castle. *Ian Allan Library*

Right: Looking south from Long Arch bridge, we see 2-8-0 No 84 (now No 13804) working hard to lift a freight out of the valley towards Combe Down. This will be some time in the 1930s. *LGRP*

Left: Round the corner from Midford goods yard, Tucking Mill (or Combe Vale) Viaduct, over the Horsecombe Brook, was rebuilt in 1894 for a double track which was never laid. No 698, on the down 'Pines' in the spring of 1936, is coasting down the 1 in 55 gradient with steam shut off, with a good deal of smoke coming from a fire well built-up for the hard pulling to come. *Real Photographs*

Below: Combe Down Tunnel, the main reason why the Bath end was never doubled. On Saturday 21 August 1954 the 10.28am Manchester-Bournemouth emerges from the south end and coasts down the Horsecombe Vale. It is hauled by 0-6-0s Nos 59 and 60 (now Nos 44559 and 44560), in the absence of sufficient passenger engines on one of the busiest days of the year. It was grossly incompetent management to expect enginemen to run expresses to time with these goods engines. *R. E. Toop*

Right: The ascent from Bath was at 1 in 50 from the junction. Here 2-8-0 No 86 (now No 53806) lifts a train of over 40 coal empties past the site of the Victoria Brick & Tile Co siding near Claude Avenue, with a banking engine whose steam can be seen in the distance. The print is annotated 'Smoke Arranged', meaning the photographer asked the fireman to throw a shovel of dust on the fire as they passed him. What the householder with washing hanging out nearby would have thought of that is a matter for speculation. *C. P. Walker*

Centre right: This view from the south platform of Bath station was taken in 1965 but could have been at any time (were it not for the engines). The arriving train is on the River Avon bridge. Beyond it on the left is the goods shed. On the right are the Midland engine shed and the S&D timber engine shed, the latter partly hidden by a water tower. Bladwell's timber yard siding ran down in front of those buildings and under the bridge. *E. W. J. Crawforth*

Below right: The main building of Bath station is gracefully proportioned with a classical frontage. Its dignity scorns the 'British Rail' contribution of a few posters, while the chalkboard 'NO PARKING' sums up the welcome extended by the latter organisation to potential patrons. Motoring enthusiasts will welcome an Austin A35. *E. W. J. Crawforth*

Left: In those days, even up to 1960 when this view was taken, one could wander about the yards at any locomotive depot and find oddments tucked away round the back. The last of the numerous and long-lived Johnson 0-4-4Ts was No 58086, built as No 1423 in 1900. On 2 July it was found dumped round the back of Bath shed, in one of the overflow sidings on the other side of the Riverside branch. Also there are 4-4-0 No 40698, dumped, and 4-4-0 No 40697 and 2-8-0 No 53805, stabled with steam still in them. Behind are the buildings of Stothert & Pitt, the crane makers. *D. Edmund*

Centre left: The original Somerset Central main line. Edington Junction station was renamed Edington Burtle, and lost its down platform and passing loop after the Bridgwater Railway closed to passengers in 1952.
C. G. Maggs

Below left: The buildings at Highbridge Works included this engine shed, seen in the early 20th century. The engine is Fox, Walker 0-6-0ST No 9 of 1876. The adjoining bay of the shed, without roof vents, is used for carriage servicing and is equipped with a sheerlegs and a handsome twin-burner gas lamp.
LGRP/Bucknall Collection

Right: The erecting shop at Highbridge. In the foreground are two engines stripped, an 0-6-0 on the left and 4-4-0 No 15 on the right, with their wheels standing between them. At the far end are a wheel lathe with a wheelset in position and three other lathes; also one of the little Highbridge-built shunting engines. Midway down each side is a rack with a couple of the ornamental safety-valve bonnets on top.
BR/Bucknall Collection

Below: A view from Highbridge station footbridge showing the proximity of the Works, still intact on 3 June 1954. The nearest building, the Carriage & Wagon Shop, was used as a store. The train arriving from Evercreech Junction is hauled by Midland 0-4-4T No 1423 (now No 58086). Behind the engine is a glimpse of the River Brue meandering beside the railway. *F. J. Saunders*

Above: On Saturday 15 August 1959, local families, about 40 in all, wait on Platform 5 at Highbridge to board a Saturday excursion which is going through to Burnham. The branch train waits at Platform 3. Both trains are hauled by Midland Class 3 0-6-0s, Nos 43682 and 43427 respectively. *F. J. Saunders*

Below: Looking westwards on Highbridge station in the 1950s. At the far right is the original Somerset Central terminus, Platforms 1 and 2. At the far end of Platforms 3 and 4, by the end of the footbridge, is 'A' signalbox, which has served as a mess-room since 1914. To its left a single track goes through to cross the GWR main line under the control of Highbridge Crossing box, visible underneath the footbridge. To the left the bridge continues over Platform 5 to reach the GWR station. 0-6-0 No 75 (now No 43248) waits to work the 2.20pm to Evercreech Junction. *R. E. Toop*

Above: Seen from Highbridge GWR station, one of the Saturday excursions, the only passenger trains to venture across the main line after 1951, caught in the act on 13 September 1958. The fireman on No 73 (now No 43218) looks as though he expects a Great Western train to roar up and apprehend him for his temerity. *R. E. Toop*

Below: On the way back from Highbridge Wharf with a goods, 0-6-0 No 72 (now No 43216) has just passed Highbridge 'B' box and level crossing and is about to cross the main line. The signal pulled off is for the run through to the S&D, the lower arm is for the chord line into the GWR station. Beyond is the goods shed, marked 'GWR GOODS OFFICE' with the 'G' painted out. The notice, right foreground, reads: 'WARNING keep well clear of mail bag apparatus on trains.' The establishment with the chimney on the right is the Western Counties Brick Co. *J. R. Ainslie*

Left: Polsham station in about 1913. A level crossing, behind the camera, was worked from the main building, and a siding, off to the left, was worked by a ground frame at the far end. *LGRP*

Centre left: The intersection at Wells. The S&D branch comes in from the left. The tracks curving round on the left lead to Priory Road passenger station; those crossing to the right lead to the goods yard and Snow's timber yard. From front to back is the link to the GWR Tucker Street station, which enabled through running between Yatton and Witham. This track bridges a mill leat which passes in front of the siding on which the van stands. By the culvert is Milepost 293 — the distance from St Pancras. *J. R. Ainslie*

Below left: The Wells branch push-pull train proudly posed outside Priory Road station in May 1950: an S&D coach with engine No 58046, then 79 years old. *J. D. Mills*

Right: Four-wheel first/second class coach No 4, built at Highbridge, seen as fitted with the vacuum brake about 1880. The now-preserved No 4 replaced this one in 1886. *LGRP*

The Trains

The coaches and wagons used on the S&D were quite conventional. For its operating debut the company ordered 25 passenger coaches, comprising four first class, eight seconds, four thirds, five composites and four brake vans. The goods vehicles were 30 high-sided open wagons, 40 low-sided wagons, six flat carriage trucks, 12 timber bolster wagons and four horseboxes. All these were supplied by the firms John Perry of Bristol, Joseph Wright of Birmingham and Rowland Brotherhood of Chippenham: examples of the small firms, descendants of the old coach builders, which supplied the railways until eliminated by amalgamation and the bigger railways' resolve to build their own stock. The S&D adopted this course and built its coaches and wagons at Highbridge as soon as the shops were working in 1862.

The coaches were entirely according to the common standards of the day: arc-roofed timber bodies with compartment accommodation. Their appointments were among the best in the country — when the LSWR moved in after the lease of 1875, it found the third-class seating equal to its own seconds. There were no corridor or catering vehicles, the coaches for the long-distance trains which arrived over the Bath extension being provided by the Midland. New construction at Highbridge continued until 1914.

The body of first class coach No 4, built in 1886, was found serving as a cricket pavilion in Templecombe, and six-wheeled thirds Nos 98 and 114 were identified incorporated into holiday homes on the coast. They have been recovered for rebuilding by the Somerset & Dorset Railway Trust.

The first engines purchased in 1861 were eight 2-4-0s built by George England & Co. There were finally 20 of this type, of which one came from Edward Bury & Co and two from the Vulcan Foundry. The last two England engines were from a batch ordered by the South Eastern Railway to its own design, but which it had refused to accept. Most of them were sold

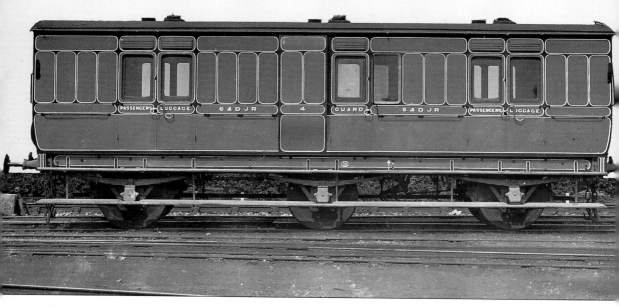

PASSENGERS LUGGAGE   S & D J R   4   GUARD   S & D J R   PASSENGERS LUGGAGE

in part-exchange for more powerful engines in the 1870s, although one, No 8, which was supplied as a tank engine for shunting, was working, very much modernised, until 1928. The Vulcans, delivered in 1866, lasted until 1914. One of the Englands, No 11, a saddle tank bought in 1863 for working the Wells branch, was exhibited by England at the Hyde Park Exhibition of 1862 and arrived specially painted in a brilliant blue livery.

When the Bath extension was undertaken, six-coupled engines were bought. Six were tender engines from John Fowler of Leeds and nine were saddle tanks built by Fox, Walker of Bristol. The latter are chiefly remembered because Nos 5 and 7 were hauling the two trains in the Radstock disaster of 1876. They were robust, powerful machines and were all kept in service by the LMS, latterly for shunting, until the big clear-out of 1930.

On taking control, the Joint Committee at once restocked with engines to standard Midland designs, although they were all built by contractors as the works at Derby was then overwhelmed by the rapid expansion of the company. Nine 0-4-4Ts were built by Avonside Engine Co of Bristol and six 0-6-0s by Neilson of Glasgow. From then on, any temporary

shortage of motive power could be met by borrowing from Midland stock. However, the line was expected to be self-sufficient and by 1890 had acquired 22 more 0-6-0s and four more 0-4-4Ts, all from the Vulcan Foundry.

In 1879 Highbridge Works began a practice of not only overhauling engines but reconstructing them with more modern components. New boilers were supplied from Derby and were usually larger than those replaced, so that the engines were up-rated in power and modernised in appearance. In this process Highbridge managed to incorporate its own ideas into fittings and finishings; thus even a standard Midland engine took on an S&D look. Highbridge did not have the capability to manufacture big parts like boilers, frames and wheels, but three small four-coupled tank engines, used for shunting in the Radstock area, were credited as 'built at Highbridge'. They were Nos 25A (1885), 26A and 45A (both 1895). The provenance of their components was not recorded, but there were several users of small engines in the Somerset Coalfield. In 1929 they were replaced by two Sentinel vertical-boilered geared engines, which were numbered 101 and 102 and were the last engines to be numbered in the Joint Committee independent register.

Above left: Another No 4, a six-wheel passenger brake van, built in about 1887. *BR*

Above: Six-wheel third class coach No 54, built at Highbridge in the mid-1880s. *BR*

From 1891 the Midland supplied 4-4-0s built at Derby. Although they were designed there and employed current standard parts, they were produced especially for the S&D and incorporated differences from the others, of which the principal one was the use of smaller wheels, thought to be better for climbing the gradients. Four were supplied in 1891, four in 1897, three in 1903, two in 1908, two in 1914, three in 1921 and three in 1928. These last were standard LMS Class 2Ps; they were numbered 575, 576 and 580, but were delivered as S&D Nos 44, 45 and 46 and when taken into the LMS fold became Nos 633, 634 and 635.

The oldest engine to survive World War 2 was No 62, an 0-6-0 built in 1896; nine sister engines did likewise. They were standard Class 2s, rebuilt in the 1920s to Class 3. In 1922 five standard Class 4 0-6-0s were supplied by Armstrong Whitworth. Nos 57-61, they had the distinction of continuing to carry those numbers

until the 1960s, having a '5', a '4' and another '4' added by successive owners. The last engine running in British Railways service which had carried an S&D identity was No 22, one of six standard Class 3 0-6-0Ts ordered from W. G. Bagnall & Co in 1928; she was scrapped in June 1967 as No 47313.

Now, of course, when an engine enthusiast hears 'Somerset & Dorset', he thinks '2-8-0s'. The impact of these engines in 1914 may be assessed by contrasting them with the largest Derby freight engine, the Class 4, which came out three years previously: an extra pair of coupled wheels; the firegrate increased from 21 to 28sq ft; boiler pressure up from 175 to 190psi; cylinder bore up from 20 to 21in; stroke up from 26 to 28in; and engine weight up from 49 tons to 68½ tons.

The 2-8-0s were designed by James Clayton and represented the first advance at Derby since the work of S. W. Johnson in 1876. The bigger cylinders had to be placed outside the frames. In view of the locomotives long wheelbase and the track's undulating nature, compensating levers were fitted between the front and rear pairs of coupled axles, and the coupling rods were given marine-type bushes. The brakes were equipped with blocks of a

Above left: From 1898 to 1913, Highbridge built bogie stock. In this 1930s view a three-coach set augmented by a brake third forms a down service, climbing southwards out of Midford, hauled by 0-6-0 No 59 (now No 4559). *IAL*

Left: Engine No 13, bought from from George England in 1864. This shows several improvements over the first batch of 1861, including enlarged firebox steam space, a much stronger coupling rod and a capacious sandbox on top of the boiler. The men had some difficulty keeping still for the duration of the exposure. *LPC/Bucknall Collection*

Above: This England 2-4-0, built as a tank in 1863 for working the Wells branch, was only on the S&D until 1870, when it was sold to the Admiralty. However, it was painted by the makers in a rich blue livery (and was unofficially named *Bluebottle*), which so impressed the railway staff that years later they adopted the colour as their house standard. *LPC/Bucknall Collection*

composite material produced by the Ferodo company (railway brake blocks are usually made of soft cast iron). The only weakness was the use of the standard Midland axleboxes and horns, which can be seen even by the lay eye to be small for the size of the engine and were inadequate for the prolonged pounding they took on the Mendips.

Commentators are wont to say: 'Why did Derby not build engines like these before and why, having done it, did they never produce any more?' The answer to the second part is that they never got the chance; this was 1914, remember. The answer to the first part is that Midland operating policy was that two short trains were easier to handle than one long one, and improved traffic flow was better achieved by reducing the transit time of goods than by increasing the amount of goods in transit. This was an unquestioned creed throughout the company, and, if it was at fault, onus lay in its being slow to grasp that this policy could not

be applied to the S&D. When it did it went for bigger engines, some 10 years after the other big players in the freight game.

Six engines were built by Derby and a further five were contracted to Robert Stephenson & Hawthorn in 1925. Other engines came and went but they were the solid base of the haulage effort until the run-down of the railway. Fortuitously two of them were sold to a scrap dealer when condemned in 1964 and were not broken up. No 88 was preserved by the Somerset & Dorset Railway Trust at Radstock and then on the West Somerset Railway, where it was restored to working order. No 89 was rebuilt by Mr Frank Beaumont and worked some excursions on British Railways before becoming resident at the Midland Railway Centre.

The S&D was very hard on engines, whether by virtue of the road itself or the practices of the drivers and firemen. It is important to remember that men were trained on the route, not on the engine; the fitters and boilermakers had to get to know the strengths and weaknesses of each design but they had no access to the hierarchies of the footplate or the schedules. The practice of working freights

down the Mendip gable without assisting engines placed a premium on brake performance, and more engines failed the S&D test on that score than on any other. The types tried and found wanting included the '990' class 4-4-0, the Midland Compound, the 'Flatiron' 0-6-4T, the LTSR 4-4-2T, the Ivatt Class 4 2-6-0, the GWR '5600' 0-6-2T, and the MoS 2-8-0.

The only LMS engine type of the new generation to appear on the line before World War 2 was the Class 5MT 4-6-0, which, as remarked, arrived in March 1938. However, in the autumn of 1941 they were removed, with the exception of No 5440, and for the first time the other partner provided the motive power; all 10 'S11' 4-4-0s, 'T9' 4-4-0 No 304 and 'T1' 0-4-4Ts Nos 1-6. 'Land Crab' 2-6-0s, including No 2766, also came through from the north and the 'S11s' were appropriated for jobs as far away as Leicester. Freight traffic increased enormously and the line's special 2-8-0 engines were reinforced by three of the standard Class 8Fs. Of course, during the war rolling stock went all over the place; for example, on 4 November 1940 military specials to Blandford were hauled by 'N15' 4-6-0 No 755 *The Red*

Left: England 2-4-0 No 8 was built as a well tank in 1861 for the Burnham branch. It is seen at Burnham in 1883 after rebuilding by Highbridge with a Johnson boiler, renumbered 28A. *LGRP/Bucknall Collection*

Right: No 28A was the longest-lived of the 2-4-0s and worked until 1928. This is the final version, after rebuilding in 1904. *J. E. Kite/ Bucknall Collection*

Below right: The distinctive descending line of chimney, steam dome with Salter safety valves, then spring safety valve in a brass bonnet, characterises a boiler from Derby in the reign of S. W. Johnson. This is Vulcan Foundry 2-4-0 No 20 of 1866, as rebuilt in 1881 and renumbered 16A. *A. W. Bartlett/ Bucknall Collection*

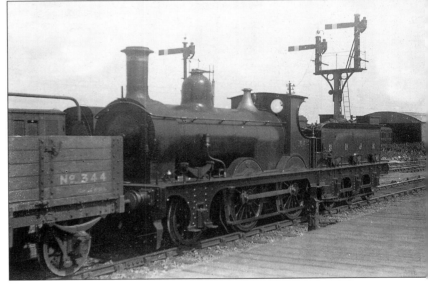

Knight and 'V' 4-4-0s Nos 928 *Stowe* and 933 *King's Canterbury*, with a 'B4' 0-4-0T to do the shunting. After the war Templecombe acquired Southern shunting engines of the 'G6' and, later, 'Z' classes.

What should have been a tremendous advance in haulage came in March 1951 when the Southern 'West Country' class 4-6-2 arrived for test runs. It happened that the long-distance expresses were drastically curtailed at the time owing to a coal shortage, but when things returned to normal on 19 March the premier train, the 'Pines Express', was rostered for a 'West Country'. Five, Nos 34040-4, were placed

at Bath depot, but that was a mistake as the class had components and servicing requirements which were quite unlike any other British steam engine, and in 1954 they were replaced by four new Standard Class 5 4-6-0s, Nos 73050-2/4. 'West Countries' continued to operate on the expresses, running from the Southern depot in Bournemouth, but being drawn from the latter's large stock did not have the S&D quality of individuality. They were noted for having to be double-headed sooner than any other type, a pair being used as early as 5 October 1951. Another Southern type used with dubious success was the

Above left: No 9, the last of the engines supplied by Fox, Walker for the Bath extension, built in 1876. The steam locomotive has not been made yet whose owners did not find the coal space to be inadequate; the rail added to the bunker is a first attempt at improving it. *LPC*

Left: Fox, Walker No 2, with a larger tank, shunting at Midsomer Norton about the turn of the century. The poses of the men are a nice graduation of their respective status and dignity. *Bucknall Collection*

Above: The first Fox, Walker 0-6-0ST was rebuilt as a tender engine in 1888 and looked like this. However in 1908 it was converted back to a saddle tank. *Bucknall Collection*

Class U 2-6-0. The first was No 31624, put on a football special to Bristol on 8 October 1948, but it broke down on the way back.

The Standard '5s' were well liked and like their predecessors, were augmented when possible by others borrowed from Bristol or further north. (Borrowed engines included, for example, Class 5MT No 44753 from Holbeck depot, Leeds, on 22 June 1957, or Carlisle-based Class 5XP No 45723 used on the Bath-Birmingham 'Pines' on 12 December 1960.) Modern Class 4 engines were also brought in. The Ivatt 2-6-0 was not highly regarded but the Standard version was popular; in 1960 Nos 75002/7/23/27 were allocated to Templecombe in place of the last of the 4-4-0s.

That takes us up to the close of the S&D story. Through all these troubled years the other old faithfuls, the 2-8-0s, had been plodding on, but in 1960 the earlier batch were taken off the books and scrapped. To take their place on the mineral hauls some LMS standard 2-8-0s were brought in, but the latter were not, it seems, trusted to deal with summer extra passenger trains as the old 'uns had done; then someone came up with another idea.

The British Railways Class 9F 2-10-0, intended to work fast freight trains, was found soon after its introduction in 1954 to be exceptionally free-running and smooth-riding, and before long the Western Region was using

its allocation on summer extra passenger trains — after all, if a Class 5 with 6ft wheels could do 80mph, then a '9F' with 5ft wheels could do 67mph. In 1958 the WR took over the S&D locomotive depots and, on checking the rolling stock running restrictions, discovered that the '9F' would be permitted over the whole of the main line. On 29 March 1960 No 92204 made a test run, with such success that for the summer season four engines of the class were temporarily based on Bath depot.

The duties initially booked for the 'Nines' were:

(1) 2.40am down freight/mail, up 'Pines Express', down 'Pines Express', 7.35pm up freight;

(2) 9.53am down passenger, 3.40pm Bournemouth-Bristol as far as Templecombe, an evening Templecombe-Bath freight.

They were allowed to haul 12 coaches unassisted over the Mendips and were used on heavy through expresses in order to avoid where possible the expense of double-heading. At the end of the summer they went to the Southern Region to work oil trains from Fawley Refinery. The allocation of four engines was repeated in the summers of 1961, 1962 and 1963. The '9Fs' were not totally Mendip-proof — on the very last day of through expresses, the '9F'-hauled 9.25am Bournemouth-Liverpool had to seek unscheduled assistance over the hill — but on the whole they formed a rousing final number to the S&D locomotive show.

Colour was yet another speciality of the trains. Almost all the early railways employed green or various shades of brown, because these were the only pigments available which withstood the elements well enough, and the Somerset Central was no exception. When Highbridge started painting, it used a dark green. In 1875 the Midland imposed its own colour, which was then a light green, and changed to the famous crimson lake in 1883. In 1886 the brilliant blue for which the line is best known was adopted for both engines and coaching stock. Vehicles coming in from the Midland would still be in the crimson livery. The blue scheme died with Highbridge Works in 1930, when all coaches became crimson and

Left: All the Fox, Walker engines except No 8 lasted into the LMS era; this is No 1 as LMS No 1500, at Radstock in 1930. *LPC/Bucknall Collection*

Right: No 26A was built at Highbridge in 1895, for shunting the Radstock collieries. *W. L. Good/ Bucknall Collection*

Centre right: No 45A, also built at Highbridge in 1895, was said to include parts of an engine built by Slaughter, Gruning of Bristol in 1882; probably No 26A's origin was similar. This shows it at Radstock shed, with a row of cattle wagons beyond. *LGRP/ Bucknall Collection*

Below right: No 101, one of two Sentinel engines bought in 1929 to replace the Radstock shunters. *LPC/IAL*

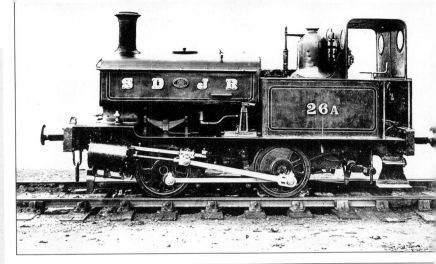

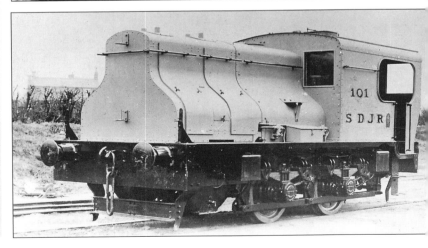

engines changed to LMS black. However, Southern green, LNER teak and GWR brown and cream stock appeared on through workings and excursions. During World War 2 coaches were (when painted at all) painted brown. British Railways made a decisive change by painting all corridor coaches red and cream and compartment stock all-over red, until 1956 when a sort of dull crimson called 'maroon' appeared. All these were hauled by black, or to be more specific, soot-coated engines. The 'West Counties' in 1951 reintroduced dark green, but they were the only green engines regularly seen on the line until Swindon Works started painting mixed-traffic types green in 1957. The standard of cleaning declined after 1960, inevitably. It is immensely time-consuming and time costs money — wastes money if there is no evidence that the customers value it — and when it was taxpayers' money there would probably have been an outcry if huge amounts of it were devoted to cosmetic activities. To the end, Bath depot achieved wonders in turning out smart engines for high-profile jobs; but that was the result of a dedication which money cannot buy.

Above: The collieries had their own shunting engines; this is Peckett No 1041, supplied new in 1906 to Coalpit Heath Colliery and named *Lord Salisbury*. It is seen working at Norton Hill on 24 March 1960. *E. W. J. Crawforth*

Above right: No 10, the first 0-4-4 passenger tank engine supplied by Avonside in 1877. This was taken after 1891 when a cab had been fitted. *LPC/IAL*

Right: Avonside 0-4-4T No 11 on passenger duty, possibly with a down train at Radstock. Visible in the cab are the regulator and reverser handle, this being the driver's side. On the signalbox, the signalman has hung a target with a cross on it above a window, which is an indication to the S&T lineman that his block instruments, telegraphs etc are all working correctly. *Bucknall Collection*

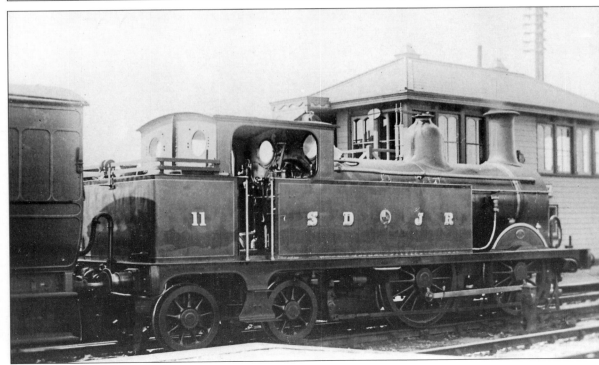

Left: When the LMS rationalised the stock in 1930 it replaced the S&D 0-4-4Ts with Midland engines of the same type. No 1408 is outside Bath shed. *LGRP/IAL*

Below left: Midland 0-4-4T No 58047, standing at Highbridge after arriving from Evercreech on 22 August 1951. The tanks have not yet lost the paint applied by their previous owner. *A. G. Newman*

Above right: 2-4-0 No 17 was one of a pair built by George England in 1865 for the South Eastern Railway but not delivered. This view at Blandford in the 1880s shows it with a Midland boiler. The 4ft 6in diameter leading wheel is very unusual in British practice. *Bucknall Collection*

Centre right: No 16, of the first batch of 4-4-0s built for the line at Derby in 1891. They were basically to the standard Midland design but had coupled wheels of 5ft 9in diameter. They were fitted with the latest gadget, steam sanding. *LGRP/ Bucknall Collection*

Below right: The S&D, like many companies, uprated its engines by installing larger boilers at each general overhaul. No 17 of the 1891 batch is shown with the first replacement boiler of 1904. It features a pair of Ramsbottom-type safety valves in place of the three valves used by Johnson. *W. L. Good/ Bucknall Collection*

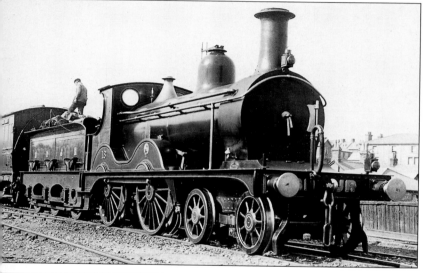

Left: On the second rebuilding, in 1908-11, the 1891 4-4-0s received this distinctive boiler, with its dome on the front ring of the barrel. No 17 is about to start from Bournemouth West with a train of S&D bogie coaches. *LGRP/ Bucknall Collection*

Centre left: 4-4-0 No 18, one of the Derby-built batch of 1891, in original condition at Blandford. This angle shows how tall and thin the locomotives of that period are in comparison with coaching stock; the tender springs are outside the body and still leave room for a gangway, while the cab side sheets only just clear the wheels. Just visible on the tender is the passenger communication cord which when pulled rings a bell in the cab. *LGRP/IAL*

Below left: No 18 was one of the engines brought into the LMS stock list when Highbridge Works was closed down. Taken on 5 July 1930, this shows it carrying LMS No 301, standing at Highbridge shed. It was scrapped in 1931. *H. C. Casserley*

Above right: A 4-4-0 in action, on a down train approaching Mill Down, north of Blandford, in 1898. No 14, built at Derby in 1897, is hauling five six-wheel coaches with a brake at each end plus two four-wheel brake vans. *LGRP/Bucknall Collection*

Right: 4-4-0 No 68, built in Derby in 1897. The superb finish and paintwork, in the blue livery, are apparent. In the cab, the control handles and even the boiler backhead are also spotless. Prominent are the regulator, two injector steam handles and, by the far wall, the vacuum brake ejector. *Bucknall Collection*

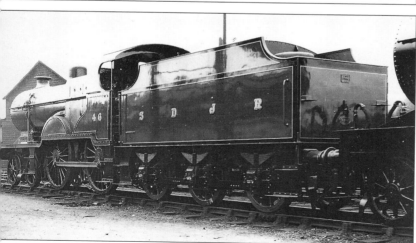

Above: 4-4-0 No 78 was supplied by Derby in 1907 and followed the latest Midland design, with 6ft wheels as a concession to the heavy gradients of the S&D. *LGRP/Bucknall Collection*

Centre left: In due course the surviving engines received the largest standard boilers introduced by R. M. Deeley. This is No 77, built in 1907, as rebuilt in 1926. It is seen at Bath in 1928, with the fireman climbing aboard after coupling up to a train. The building behind is the office and entrance to the bonded store. *J. E. Kite/Bucknall Collection*

Below left: The last locomotive supplied by Derby to the S&D as a separate entity was 4-4-0 No 46, of 1928. This was a standard engine of the type then being built in quantity for the LMS and can be seen to have left-hand drive. The cylinder on the bogie shows that bogie wheel brakes were fitted, as was the vogue at this time until it was realised that the extra braking was not worth the wear and tear so caused. *Real Photographs/IAL*

Above: No 67, a Midland standard 7ft 4-4-0 built in 1921. These engines proved that small wheels are not essential for work on steep gradients and were rated at 212 tons over the Bath extension. This engine was scrapped in 1953 as BR No 40324. As No 41 in about 1928, she is running into Broadstone with the up 'Pines Express'; a four-coach LMS restaurant set contrasts with the two S&D coaches tacked on the back. The tracks behind at a higher level are the original Southampton & Dorchester main line to Hamworthy Junction.
Real Photographs/IAL

Below: The same engine as in the previous view, coming cautiously down the hill towards Bath Junction with the 'Pines Express'. The train on this occasion is formed of Midland coaches, the first two being 1921 stock, followed by two of clerestory type.
Real Photographs/IAL

Above: 4-4-0 No 68, built at Derby in 1921 and scrapped in 1951 as BR No 40325. This view, taken at Highbridge, is clearly posed, with the crew in clean shirts and ties, but they left an oil feeder on the side and the general cleanliness is not up to prewar standard. *LPC/Bucknall Collection*

Below: By 1960 the 4-4-0s were becoming surplus. No 40537, built in 1899, is seen at the end of the line in Templecombe on 24 March. This view was taken from the bridge leading to the depot. *E. W. J. Crawforth*

Above right: The LMS replaced the older passenger engines with standard Class 2P 4-4-0s. Here is No 699, built in 1932, lifting the down 'Pines Express' out of Midford in 1938, with a splendid clear exhaust and plenty of steam. *Real Photographs/IAL*

Below right: In the summer season the 'Pines' became too heavy for one 4-4-0. Nos 696 and 692 tackle the climb out of Midford in 1936. The GWR Limpley Stoke-Camerton line can be seen running along the centre of the valley in the background. *Real Photographs/IAL*

Above: No 20, the second 0-6-0 supplied by John Fowler in 1874, standing forlorn at Highbridge, in its final form with a Midland Deeley boiler. The first 0-6-0s were eventually disposed of in 1928. *LPC/IAL*

Below: Most of the S&D 0-6-0s were of this type, a standard design for the period in the Midland pattern. This is No 27, supplied by Vulcan Foundry in 1881. The immaculate finish is marred only by an ooze of limescale from a firebox mudhole door. The serious mien of the driver, fireman, foreman and shunter is appropriate for men whose work puts them at the very forefront of technology. *LPC/IAL*

Above: 0-6-0s were used on passenger work. No 62 is on an up train approaching Blandford: 15 assorted four- and six-wheelers. This engine was built at Derby in 1896 and had the Midland pattern boiler from new. *LGRP/Bucknall Collection*

Below: No 63, built in 1896 at Derby, worked through two wars and was scrapped in 1947 as No 3198. It is heading south from Blandford in about 1898. The train comprises a six-wheel brake, a composite, a third, two through coaches from the Midland — a bogie clerestory and a 12-wheel composite — and a four-wheel brake. *LGRP/Bucknall Collection*

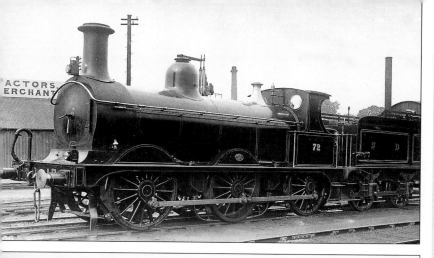

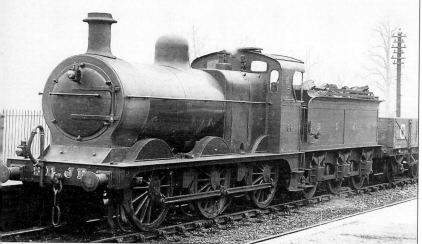

Left: No 72, built in 1902 by Neilson Reid to the Midland standard design, became British Railways No 43216 and, the last survivor of the small S&D 0-6-0s, was scrapped in 1962. *LPC/Bucknall Collection*

Centre left: From the mid-1920s the remaining S&D engines were fitted with Belpaire pattern boilers to keep them in conformity with the parent company's engines. No 66, built at Derby in 1896, is seen standing in Wellow station some time between 1920 and 1930. It is either shunting or standing on the wrong line waiting for a following train to pass. *Real Photographs/IAL*

Below left: The final appearance of an 1896 Derby engine; No 65 (now No 43204) posed at Derby after an overhaul on 25 March 1952. It was scrapped in 1956. *R. J. Buckley*

Above: From the little 0-6-0s to this would have been a startling change on any railway; for Derby, with its reputation for artistic lineaments and comparatively light construction, to produce this 2-8-0 was incredible. For reliability, power and braking they were not surpassed by any other locomotive of their size. This is No 80 as turned out from Derby Works in 1914. *BR/Bucknall Collection*

Below: Unfortunately for the S&D men, their splendid new engines were snatched away on completion, by the Midland, on the pretext that there was a war on, and were put to use on its own main line. No 85 is passing Elstree with a haul of return coal empties. *LPC/Bucknall Collection*

Above: No 85 finally made it to the S&D and is seen here at Radstock. The hardy men of the Mendips clearly scorned the protection of the rear cab roof and dispensed with it on the first overhaul. *LGRP/Bucknall Collection*

Below: No 90, last of the second batch of 2-8-0s supplied by Robert Stephenson & Hawthorn in 1925. In these the boiler diameter was increased from 4ft 8in to 5ft 3in. This was found not to produce appreciably more steam, so when replacements were needed the smaller version was used. Another change from the first batch was from right-hand to left-hand drive. *LPC*

Above: No 86, just finished, was exhibited by Stephenson's at the Stockton & Darlington Centenary celebration in 1925. It is seen in company with the latest GNR 2-8-0. On the running plate is a model of the original locomotive, built a century before by the same company for the other S&D. *IAL*

Below: From 1930 to 1932 the 2-8-0s were numbered 9670-80 inclusive. This is No 82 on 9 June 1930, with the fixing holes for its old numberplate visible above the new number, in Bath shed yard. Behind are the sand dryer and a sheerlegs over the track into the repair bay. *H. C. Casserley*

Above: In 1938 No 90, carrying its LMS number 13810, lifts a down freight, mostly loaded with coal, up the gradient from Radstock. The plume of steam from the safety valves and absence of smoke show that the locomotive is well equal to the job. *IAL*

Below: In final form with a small boiler, No 90 (now No 53810) stands in Midsomer Norton station waiting to proceed northwards with a freight on 12 April 1958. Coupled in front is LMS 0-6-0T No 47557, one of the Radstock shunters, and the photographer reports that this engine accompanied the train in order to draw wagons across to the down line during shunting movements on the way. *R. E. Toop*

Right: In 1948 the 2-8-0s were renumbered for a third time. This is No 82 at Derby Works, fresh from an overhaul in 1950s BR plain black livery as No 53802. *Author's Collection*

Centre right: An order made on behalf of the Joint Committee in 1922 was for five Midland Class 4 0-6-0s from Armstrong Whitworth. This shows them ready to leave the company's Scotswood Works. One may deduce from their hats that the man on the near engine is an erecting shop foreman and the one on the ground a director. *LGRP/Bucknall Collection*

Below: Examining the five AW engines for hot bearings on their arrival on the S&D. The engine hauling them is Midland Class 3 No 3604. *Bucknall Collection*

Above: 0-6-0 No 60 of the Armstrong Whitworth batch at work, piloting 4-4-0 No 45 on an up train at Radstock on 21 May 1929. They are passing under the bridge which carries the Tyning Colliery branch. *H. C. Casserley*

Below: Other Class 4 0-6-0s were used on the line. No 44102 was based on the S&D from the early 1950s until closure. Here it is at Cole on 6 July 1954, with a set of vintage coaches, augmented by an LMS coach at the rear. *H. Gordon Tidey*

Above: One of the first 'Black Five' Class 5MT 4-6-0s on the line was No 5440, and it remained until 1958. Shortly after Nationalisation the locomotive stands in Bournemouth West station with an express, probably the 'Pines Express', which at that time did not carry its name. *D. Sutton Collection*

Below: No 5440 (now No 45440) again, hauling a local in October 1954; seen pulling up the 1 in 50 incline from Bath to Combe Down Tunnel. The viewpoint is Maple Grove Bridge, just north of Devonshire Tunnel. *R. Russell*

Above: From 1952 the 'Black Fives' were augmented by four new BR Standard Class 5s. On 31 March 1956 the up 'Pines Express', its LMS coaches in pristine BR red and cream livery, comes out of Combe Down Tunnel and over the bridge at Watery Bottom. The engines are Nos 73052 and 44917. *I. Peters*

Left: Midland standard 0-6-0Ts were used for shunting. No 47542, LMS-built in 1927, is stabled at Templecombe shed on 23 May 1959. *J. C. Haydon*

Above: When from time to time the South Western had to help out with motive power, the type supplied was usually the 'T9' 4-4-0. On the evening of 15 May 1956 No 30706 of Bournemouth depot was on the 7.5pm Bath–Bournemouth (6.2pm from Bristol). On the right No 40563 shunts the stock of the 6.3pm arrival from Templecombe. *R. Bullock*

Below: A most unusual sight was 'T9' No 30120 on the Templecombe piloting job, seen here leaving Bath assisting a 'Standard 5' on the 'Pines Express'. They are passing the divergence of the goods yard sidings, with the engine shed on the far side. Service on the S&D is a less-celebrated part of this famous preserved engine's career. *J. K. Sanders*

Above: Another Southern type occasionally seen on the line was the 'U' class express passenger 2-6-0. No 31624 is piloting 'Black Five' No 44839 on the down 'Pines Express' in May 1950, passing Templecombe No 2 Junction. *J. B. Heyman*

Left: Great Western territory? Yes, this is Templecombe on 2 December 1961. On the right pannier tank No 4691 comes in with a northbound freight and on the left No 3795 waits to haul it back into Templecombe Upper. *G. A. Richardson*

Above: The practice of using 0-6-0 engines for all services on the Highbridge branch was continued by the Western Region, using its own '2251' class. No 2218 waits at Glastonbury with the 1.15pm Evercreech Junction-Highbridge in August 1964. The locomotive has no numberplates and has not been cleaned for years. A GPO van on the platform exchanges mail. In the foreground are two water cans, probably used for delivering water supplies to Pennard Crossing keeper's house. *P. Strong*

Below: As a personal indulgence, two friends of the author at Bournemouth West. This view of British Railways 2-10-0 No 92220 *Evening Star* ready to leave with the 3.40pm to Bath on 4 October 1963 brings to an end the line of Somerset & Dorset locomotives, and indeed symbolises the end of the line for the railway itself. *E. W. J. Crawforth*

Working Wrinkles

One of the first things considered by the new owners in 1876 was line capacity, which was clearly far below the traffic offering. More powerful locomotives brought some improvement, as did a Midland-style control system, but eventually it had to be faced: the line must be doubled. This was a costly task, as there was little or no provision in the original works for widening.

The first section tackled was Templecombe to Evercreech Junction in 1884, extended to Evercreech New in 1886 and to Shepton Mallet in 1888. Radstock to Binegar was doubled in 1885. Shepton Mallet to Binegar was done in 1892 and Radstock to Midford in 1894. Some work was done as far as Combe Down Tunnel, and Tucking Mill Viaduct was widened, but double track was not laid past the middle of Midford Viaduct. At the south end, doubling started at Blandford in 1901 and ended when Bailey Gate to Corfe Mullen Junction was converted to conventional double line working in 1905. The Corfe Mullen cut-off was built for a double track but remained single.

Besides the cutting and banking, every bridge had to be extended and new tunnels bored at Winsor Hill and Chilcompton,

Above left: Doubling the line through Spetisbury in about 1895. Comparison with the view on page 31 shows that the formation on the left side is being widened and levelled. The old signal is in the 'clear' position, the bar edge-on to us. *LGRP/Bucknall Collection*

Left: A down goods train climbing the grade into Combe Down Tunnel in 1920. The engine is No 49, built by Neilson in 1884. The first vehicle is a cattle wagon; the practice was to slosh lime wash over them at intervals as a sort of disinfectant. The second wagon belongs to the Lancashire & Yorkshire Railway, showing how far wagons were apt to wander in those days. Next are two vans, a timber-framed one and a more modern steel-framed one. *LGRP/Bucknall Collection*

fortunately only 132yd and 66yd long respectively. The Joint Committee wished to double the whole line, and it might well have done Templecombe to Blandford, which would have been less expensive than the northern part. Alternatively, it might even have been better to concentrate all the resources on the northern end and double it through from Midford to Bath, which was the most difficult section to work. A master plan to bypass the problem tunnels of Devonshire and Combe Down was trotted out in 1943, 1947 and again in 1958, but each time the accountants frowned and it was put away again.

An urgent reform of the Joint era was to the signalling arrangements. The earliest signals were to the pattern of the mentor companies, viz the LSWR in the south and the Bristol & Exeter in the north. The latter used the Brunel 'disc and crossbar' signals, generally recognised as the first signals to give a positive Danger or Clear indication. The purpose of such signals was to show whether a station was clear for the train to enter; despatch of trains was by verbal instruction from the stationmaster who received his orders by telegraph from a central controller, who was actually located at Glastonbury. This was later supplemented by a local block telegraph network so that staff might know, even if the controller did not, whether their section had a train in it. This system only ever produced two collisions but relied too much on individual infallibility, so it was replaced by proper interlocked signals and single line control using the Tyer electric tablet system. Some of the instruments installed in 1878 continued in use until 1950.

So that nonstop trains need not come down to dead slow in order to exchange tablets, Alfred Whitaker developed a mechanical exchanger which was installed throughout in 1904. The principle was simple: a metal version of the hands which held and caught the tablets. The trick was making the arms movable so they could be swung inboard

when not in use (and the ground arm had to swing in very quickly after the exchange as it was dangerously close to the passing coaches), but be strong enough to grab the tablet at up to 60mph. The first ground arm was balanced and hinged downwards, but the type finally adopted rotated, propelled through bevel gears by a weighted arm which was tripped by the impact of the arriving tablet. On units where there was no arriving tablet, that is where trains ran from a double line onto a single line, the arm was held up by a lever retained by the tablet and released when it was taken out. The driver watched the exchange, so that in the event of a miss he could put the brake on promptly; then his luckless fireman would have to walk back from where they stopped to complete the exchange in person.

Even with automatic tablet-changing, a completely nonstop run over the 71½ miles from Bath to Wimborne or Bournemouth was unknown. The holiday expresses from the north were in some cases advertised as such, but they always stopped at Evercreech Junction to take water. If an assisting engine was provided over the Mendips, it was attached or detached while the train engine was watering. They also stopped at Poole, if only because you had to negotiate its curve and level crossings so slowly that there would be little gain in not stopping. Most also stopped at Blandford and Broadstone, and some at Shepton Mallet.

With respect to local passenger traffic, the line was largely worked in two parts, with Templecombe forming a terminus in both directions. Even in its heyday only four or five stopping trains ran right through. Most freight trains ran to Evercreech Junction, where they were remarshalled. The engines worked there from Bath or Bournemouth, turned and went back, so through portions went forward behind

another engine. Those freights which ran through Evercreech had to stop in Templecombe Lower yard for examination, during which the engine was usually changed. The 'Branch' — the line from Evercreech Junction to Highbridge, Bridgwater and the Wells section — was self-contained, passenger trains working from Evercreech Junction or, in later years, Templecombe.

A peculiarity, which will be seen in every picture in this book showing a moving train, was the positioning of the headlamps on the engine. A train classification code was one of many national standards created by the companies, through their co-ordinating body the Railway Clearing House, and generally used by about 1910, but the S&D never got around to complying with that. Its code was: any passenger train, lamps at the top and left buffer; any freight, top and right buffer; light engine, top lamp only.

Excursions were always a feature of operation; soon after the opening through to Wimborne the S&D was advertising day trips to Dorchester — the objective being not so much sightseeing as attending the market. The company issued special reduced tickets to market traders, and also to those attending 'Meetings of Religious Bodies' and 'Golf Meetings (competitors and certified members of Golf Clubs)'. August Bank Holiday 1876, the day that culminated in the Radstock collision, saw 17 extra trains over the main line. The inhabitants of Burnham were offered an afternoon excursion to Wells, leaving at 12.40pm and getting home at 9pm, for a fare of 1s 6d, while the people of Wells could escape the influx by joining a similar excursion to Burnham. Both the railway and the Cardiff-Bristol Channel Steamship Co ran rail-and-ship excursions via Burnham; a typical example from 1880 was a day trip to Ilfracombe, for

Above left: A close-up of the Wells branch train on 21 April 1951. There are three wagons, two rickety-looking wooden opens and a modern steel mineral wagon. The coach is push-pull fitted, as is the engine. No 58086 was on this job for many years. *J. D. Mills*

Left: An excursion organised by Ian Allan Ltd on 25 April 1954. The train is Southern Railway Maunsell stock on holiday from its usual job of carrying Kent Coast commuters, and the engine is from Bath. Seen here at Evercreech Junction on the way to Templecombe, whence the train returned direct to London. *E. D. Bruton*

Above: Understandably, most photographers worked only in warm weather. This represents the winter face of the Mendips. The date is 15 January 1963, the location is near Wincanton, and the photographer notes that the down train, headed by 0-6-0 No 58 (now No 44558), was running 2hr late. The lineside furniture is of interest. On the left is a 'C' sign for a temporary speed restriction and to the right is the 'T' sign for the end of it in the other direction. On a post is a GWR illuminated permanent speed-restriction sign and below it the cut-out '40' is a BR non-illuminated replacement. *Rev R. T. Hughes*

which you had to be at Bath or Bournemouth station for a 6am start.

A snapshot of the basic service on the line is provided by the programme for 20 May 1910, the day when the funeral of King Edward VII took place and a minimum service was run, primarily to take the dairy produce. That could not, of course, be abandoned, whatever day it was. On the main line two down trains and one up ran carrying passengers, milk and perishables, one passengers only and one milk only:

Bath dep	7.0am	5.30pm
Bournemouth arr	11.11	9.20
Bournemouth dep	7.5am	6.52pm pass
Bath arr	11.35	10.22
Wimborne dep	1.35pm milk	
Bath arr	5.55	

On the Branch a morning and evening train ran each way between Burnham and Evercreech Junction, taking an hour and a quarter on the way. There were also four trips each way on the five-minute run between Burnham and Highbridge and an evening train from

Highbridge to Templecombe and back. Wells
had four services from Glastonbury, the
running time being 15min down and 14min up.
The Bridgwater Railway also had four round
trips to Edington Junction, the running time
being 15min.

For comparison, here are the corresponding
main line times in 1947:

Bath dep	6.55am	7pm
Bournemouth arr	11.3	10.44
Bournemouth dep	6.48am	3.30pm
Bath arr	11.5	6.54

Through expresses were much faster. In 1874
the 12.35pm from Bath was in Bournemouth by
3.25, while the 10.20am up took only 2hr 40min.
In 1904 the predecessor of the 'Pines Express'
took 2hr 2min down and 2hr 3min up. In 1934
the 'Pines' took 2hr 17min down and 2hr 9min
up; in 1954 it took 2hr 32min down and 2hr
11min up.

Double-heading was always quoted as the
'S&D disease' which made it uneconomic to
work, which of course was just a specious
excuse for lack of investment. It was much
easier to go on for years complaining about
high operating costs than to persuade
shareholders, or latterly taxpayers, to stump up
the cash for better facilities. In fact the engines
provided were adequate when they were
introduced. Only as trains grew more luxurious
and heavier were they overloaded, at first on
peak holiday services, then gradually more
often until double-heading became the rule;
then the owners were cajoled or coerced into
introducing more powerful engines. This
progression continued until the arrival of the
ultimate power unit, the BR Class 9F 2-10-0,
which could haul unaided the biggest train the
S&D could accommodate.

Assisting engines were most often needed
over the northern half, from, as remarked
above, Evercreech Junction. The job was one for
Templecombe depot; on a Saturday it would

Left: This display of dahlias, albeit out of focus in this shot, could only be at Midsomer Norton, the station that consistently won garden competitions in Midland, LMS and BR days. Midland 0-6-0T No 47275 shunts coal from Norton Hill Colliery. This engine, built in 1924, was a contemporary of the S&D's own machines of the same type. The shunter is riding on the engine but he has left his pole across the buffer-stocks of the front wagon. *D. Cross*

turn out a bunch of pilot engines which would run up to Evercreech to await the string of northbound through expresses. Assisting these to Bath, they would be in time to pilot the corresponding southbound trains. The situation at Bath in the middle of the day, with the pairs of engines which had come up the S&D to turn and refuel at the same time as the other pairs which had come down from the north, demanded not so much shunters as master chess players. A passenger engine was naturally preferred for piloting, but if they ran short they would use the freight engines whose jobs were suspended on these busy days, so a relief express to the Midlands was often seen piloted by a Class 4F 0-6-0 or even an 0-6-0 tank engine. The 2-8-0s were also used for this work and were highly valued, for although not fast they would plod imperturbably along regardless of the load. The last of the 4-4-0s were used for piloting in the 1961 season. Although they were only 30 years old, the magnitude of change in that period was such that by then the appearance of engines of this type on Class A trains was exceptional, especially when the same train was hauled later in its journey by a 2,500hp diesel.

Freight trains were not double-headed but banked in the rear, from Bath to the entrance of Combe Down Tunnel, from Radstock to Masbury summit and from Evercreech Junction to Masbury. The banker was not coupled up and could drop off the rear of the train on seeing it safely over the summit. It then had to return the way it had come, and, since Masbury summit did not have a crossover, it could only do that by running 'wrong line'. At Binegar and

Winsor Hill boxes a special tablet was provided, functioning in the same way as a single-line tablet, which the banker driver picked up as he passed and was his authority to return in the wrong direction without the formality of a written Wrong Line Order. Indeed, it was better as it was positively interlocked and the signalman could not clear his signal until it was brought back. A similar staff was used at Bath Junction and locked the signalling so that another train could not be admitted until both the tablet and the banking staff were back in their instruments.

Another place where assistance was provided was the 1 in 60 incline from Poole to Parkstone on the South Western main line. Here trains of all classes were banked in the rear from Poole to Branksome if needed. Banking was also available out of Wimborne, but curiously, engines were normally expected to get over the equally-severe Corfe Mullen cut-off without assistance.

The most difficult part of the line was the Bath Junction-Midford single line section. Commencing half a mile from the stops in the terminus, it was 3 miles 70 chains long. It rose almost continuously at 1 in 50, through the 447yd Devonshire Tunnel, to the end of Combe Down Tunnel, whose 1,829yd were nearly all on a descent at 1 in 100. The descent continued at 1 in 50, 100, 55 and 160 to Midford, finishing at 1 in 330 down across the viaduct, where it changed to 1 in 60 up. It was particularly unpleasant on a double-headed up train, when an engine probably down to the dust in the bottom of the tender had to be kept at work through the mile-long narrow hole under Combe Down, its crew obliged to inhale the exhaust of another engine in front. As an example of the occupation of the section, we have chosen the summer 1937 timetable. Freight trains were allowed 14min (including a minute between Bath Single Line Junction and the yard, which we will count as lever-pulling time). In that time a banking engine, if taken, would go halfway and come back. Passenger trains took 10min, plus an extra minute or two if calling at Midford station, whose platform lay within the single line. On Mondays to Fridays, in 24 hours 54 trains were scheduled, and there was actually something in the section for 48% of

Left: One of the disc-and-bar signals used in the early years as a result of the political and practical support from the Bristol & Exeter Railway. It was pivoted merely by sitting in two hoops against the stanchion, pulled off by the chain and restored by the weighted arm. The lamp showed in the 'Stop' position only. *LGRP/Bucknall Collection*

Below left: A single-line tablet, for the Corfe Mullen Junction-Broadstone section, and its leather pouch. *IAL*

those 24 hours; 31 of them ran in the 12 hours 7am-7pm, occupying 50% of that time. That does not include any extra trains or trips to the Co-op's and May's sidings. The trains were pretty well spread over the 24 hours, but that is the timetable, not what actually happened when services were disrupted by late-running from the north. On Saturdays, when most daytime freights were withdrawn to make way for through expresses, the total was 64 trains and 53%, and for 7am-7pm 37 trains and 56%. The Bath-Midford section was *booked* to be continuously occupied for all but 16min from 1pm to 3.15. That adds up to a busy railway by any standards, and, if any piece of line deserved improvement, this one did. It would not have been all that difficult, either. From Midford add a curve down to join the GWR branch, which would be up-graded to Limpley Stoke, where a northward curve would be added to the junction to take trains through Bathampton to Bath Spa. A new connection would be needed west of Bath to the Midland line — perhaps a mile of new work in total. This would have added distance but would have been so much easier to work and would have transformed the S&D by linking it direct to the GWR main lines. The reasons it was not done were that it would have entailed spending money to encourage potential business rather than merely reacting to an existing overload, and abandoning established patterns of usage; both were utter anathema to railway management in the mid-20th century.

In that summer of 1937 Bath station's scheduled passenger trains were mostly locals to and from Bristol or Clifton Down: 19 arriving and 18 departing. There were eight locals heading south over the S&D and eight arriving

Above: Tablet exchanging in the traditional way. The signalman at Sturminster Newton hands a tablet to an up express in the year 1898. He is holding it incorrectly; you should hold the tablet you are giving out in a backhand grip so that it is pulled out of your hand rather than driven into it. *LGRP/Bucknall Collection*

from it. The through trains, reversing in the station, were:

8.46am		Bristol-Bournemouth
10am	MFO	Bournemouth-Sheffield
10.35am		Bournemouth-Manchester 'Pines'
9.35am	MFO	Sheffield-Bournemouth
10am		Manchester-Bournemouth 'Pines'
10.40am		Lincoln-Bournemouth
7.38pm		Bournemouth-Bristol.

In addition, the 2.15am parcels from Birmingham, the 9.50pm return train and the 2.40am freight/mail to Bournemouth used the passenger platforms. On the goods side there were 16 timetable paths available on to the S&D and 13 from it, although these were not necessarily all used. There were 13 departures for the north and 10 incoming; most of these went to and from Westerleigh marshalling yard, with the important exception of the 1.30am fitted No 1 freight from Birmingham Exchange, which arrived at 7.35am and proceeded over

the S&D at 7.50am, and the return working which came in at 8.45pm and went forward at 9.15pm to Birmingham Lawley Street.

On a 1937 summer Saturday the locals and freights were curtailed to free paths for through trains, 23 of them:

11pm (Friday)	Bournemouth-Manchester
10.15pm (Friday)	Manchester-Bournemouth
8.55pm (Friday)	Bradford-Bournemouth
8.46am	Bristol-Bournemouth
6.20am	Derby-Bournemouth
9.45am	Bournemouth-Lincoln
10am	Bournemouth-Bradford
10.20am	Bournemouth-Liverpool
10.35am	Bournemouth-Manchester
9.22am	Sidmouth-Derby
9.55am	Walsall-Bournemouth
10.24am	Derby-Sidmouth
7.35am	Bradford-Bournemouth
11.40am	Bournemouth-Sheffield
9.55am	Nottingham-Bournemouth
9.55am	Manchester-Bournemouth
9.40am	Liverpool-Bournemouth
10.35am	Nottingham-Bournemouth
1.50pm	Bournemouth-Birmingham
10.58am	Bradford-Bournemouth
2.45pm	Bournemouth-Derby
5pm	Bournemouth-Birmingham
7.38pm	Bournemouth-Bristol.

Above: Over 50 years later, the same ritual is carried out at Highbridge. In this case the tablet is handed to the departing train as it passes East box. The train is the 4.0pm to Evercreech Junction.
R. E. Toop

Left: A Whitaker tablet-changer, showing the weight and bevel gears which turn it away from the track. This one is at Binegar and supplies a special tablet to banking engines on passing southbound freight trains, authorising them to return on the same line from Masbury summit. Because it only gives out tablets, the weight which rotates it is tripped by the removal of the same. (It is now preserved by the Somerset & Dorset Railway Trust.) In the distance the line can be seen rising at 1 in 63 on the final stretch to Masbury. The overgrown yard was the exchange point with the Oakhill Brewery line.
IAL

Above right: Approaching Templecombe No 2 Junction, the fireman of 0-6-0 No 75 (now No 43248) has his tablet on the changer ready to be taken. They are passing the old Lower station; the buildings on the right are those of the SR station. This view was taken in May 1952.
J. Davenport

On a Sunday the S&D was quiet but not quiescent. There was the through train from Bristol, at 11am from Bath and back at 7.45pm from Bournemouth, another northbound passenger/milk train in the afternoon, and three or four northbound freight workings. This left plenty of room for excursions.

Weather was a significant working hazard. Masbury summit's 811 feet does not sound high — it is only a 43-wagon goods train stood on end, for goodness' sake — but is high as railway summits go in this country and, while nothing like as cold as the northern lines, has the regrettable characteristic that, in winter, the temperature swings just above and below freezing. In this area where damp air blasts in from the Bristol Channel with ample vigour, that means sudden heavy snowfalls and lying moisture turning to ice, which plays havoc with outdoor machinery. In the winter of 1891 the whole railway was disabled from Monday 9 March to Saturday, with snowdrifts up to 15ft deep filling cuttings. The staff cleared the line by heroic efforts, such as that of Superintendent Robert Dykes, who walked four miles along the track in a blizzard to find a stranded train. January 1940 was one of the coldest spells on record, with a blizzard on the 12th which overwhelmed the LMS with 313 snow blockages. On the S&D ice build-up brought down the entire telegraph rig over the Mendips, requiring staff to work trains on the primæval time-interval system until they could make a temporary telephone line. Another bad winter was in 1962; it began snowing on Saturday 29 December and continuous snow-ploughing through the next day (there were no public services on Sundays then) failed to prevent drifting. On 3 January three trains, including the plough, were buried and it took three days to dig them out, the Mendips section being closed for a fortnight.

Everyone likes to read about disasters, but (to your disappointment) the S&D had a superb safety record. Mind you, the few serious accidents it did have were as idiosyncratic as everything else it did. The famous one was a head-on collision between two passenger trains on Bank Holiday Monday 7 August 1876. Both trains were extra excursions, running on forced paths being worked out as they went along by the Glastonbury controller who, at the time of the collision, had lost trace of both of them. The telegraph clerks at Radstock and Wellow stations, both boys acting without supervision, despatched the trains towards each other on the

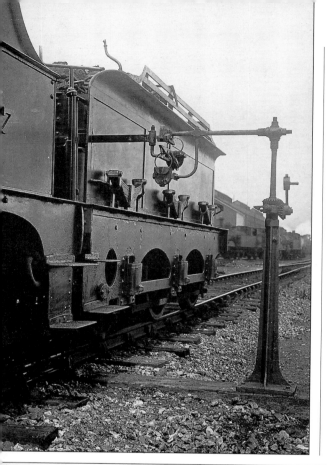

Left: An early Whitaker apparatus on test outside Highbridge Works, shown at the moment of contact. The ground arm is taking the upper tablet from the engine as the engine arm grabs the lower one. *IAL*

Above: The engine arm on 0-6-0 No 60, receiving jaws pointing to the left and giving-up holder on the right. *Author's Collection*

Below: The Bath Junction apparatus in action, giving a tablet to a summer Saturday Birmingham-Bournemouth extra, as it takes the curve onto the S&D on 1 August 1953. The fireman of 2-8-0 No 90 (now No 53810) is watching it, as is the fireman on the pilot, a Class 4 0-6-0. *P. G. Barlow*

Above: There were other designs of tablet-changer tried before the revolving arm was adopted. One was called the 'falling man' because it was pivoted to fold down after performing. In this view at Templecombe No 2 Junction on 30 June 1950, two of this type remain in situ, one each side of the front of the engine. The train is about to take the curve up to Templecombe Upper station. Three of the coaches are S&D veterans, with an LMS vehicle at the rear. The engine is LMS 4-4-0 No 568, built in 1928. According to the photographer, the mark on the cabside by the fireman's head is a 'Blue route' restriction mark applied by the Western Region, which then owned the northern half of the permanent way. *J. D. Mills*

single line without contacting each other or using the block instruments. The drivers did not query the lack of proper crossing orders; they had become resigned to the chaotic situation and, like all working men, were in no position to complain about the company's procedures. The engines, Fox, Walker 0-6-0STs Nos 5 and 7, were only damaged, but the light coaches were smashed and 12 passengers and one of the guards were killed. The accident drew unwelcome attention to a signalbox at Foxcote, erected to work the Braysdown

Colliery sidings, which was being used like an intermediate block post to divide the Radstock-Wellow section — this was illegal as only one train is allowed in a single line section. The signalman here was also a teenager, unable to read or write, not strong enough to pull over the levers and not provided with telegraph instruments or even oil for his signal lamps. He was arrested and blamed for the collision. This was one of a series of accidents in the 1870s which highlighted the rapaciousness of the railway companies and the inhumanity of the British legal system.

Another head-on collision between two goods trains took place in the Binegar-Masbury section on 3 February 1886, in consequence of the signalman forgetting one of them, as a result of which the crossing order system was finally condemned.

Not many accidents have any humorous element, but some time in about the year 1920 the company's ship *Alpha* came to grief in an embarrassing manner by Highbridge Wharf. Sitting on the bottom at low tide, she was loaded with 130 tons of flour. Unfortunately, the sticky Somerset mud held her fast while the tide rose, and she did not rise with it. The result when it reached deck level was a record-breaking batch of flour-and-water paste.

A poignant tragedy occurred on 20 November 1929. The crew of 2-8-0 No 89 were overcome by smoke as it laboured up the gradient through Combe Down Tunnel with an up freight. With no hand on the controls, the train careered down the hill, through Bath Junction, and piled up at the turn into the goods yard. The driver was killed but the fireman miraculously survived.

On 29 July 1936 another freight hauled by a 2-8-0 got out of control on the descent to Radstock and pushed the engine out past all the signals. When the crew saw ahead of them 0-6-0T No 7620 standing on the main line at Writhlington box (the successor to Foxcote), they baled out. The driver of No 7620 kept his head, jumped from his footplate, ran towards the approaching engine, climbed aboard and stopped it before the collision. Unfortunately, he left his regulator open and his fireman, misunderstanding his precipitate departure, also jumped off; then No 7620, unmanned, charged away northwards propelling eight wagons. They passed Wellow at 50mph but at Midford the wagons derailed, demolishing all the lineside furniture and sweeping the box from under the signalman's feet. No 7620, still

Above: The summer holidays crammed the line to overflowing. Here we see the Midland area of Bath shed at midday on August Bank Holiday Saturday, 31 July 1954, with engines ready to take out the expresses from the north to Bournemouth. In this view are Nos 44810, 44815, 45401, 34108 *Wincanton*, 47557, 44150 and 40527. *Rev A. G. Newman*

Above right: The 'Black Fives' were supposed to avoid the need to pilot over the Mendips and for a while they did so. In June 1938, soon after arrival, No 5432 hauls the up 'Pines Express' past Binegar with eight on, well inside its load limit. *Real Photographs*

Right: The Bulleid 'West Country' was another class which was brought in to eliminate double-heading. In the early 1950s No 34040 *Crewkerne* is on a 12-coach down 'Pines Express' and needs assistance from old faithful No 40568. They are seen passing Shoscombe & Single Hill halt. *Real Photographs*

pushing half a wagon, ran on through the tunnels and finally became derailed herself just before reaching Bath Junction.

On 19 August 1949 a mixed train from Glastonbury to Highbridge was ambling across the Somerset Levels from Ashcott to Shapwick.

Here a 2ft gauge tramway, serving the Eclipse Peat Co peat-beds, crossed the line and, invisible in the misty morning, a petrol locomotive had stalled on the crossing. The engine, 0-6-0 No 76 (by now No 3260), was derailed by the impact and rolled over into the South Drain alongside to form an instant dam. No-one was hurt and the rest of the train was removed, but with the railway track as the only firm base in an expanse of bog, there was nowhere to prop a crane to achieve the lift necessary to extract the engine. Eventually it was cut up on the spot.

The story of the Somerset & Dorset Railway does not end with these views from the past, for the enterprising spirit which created it is very much alive in the present. The Somerset & Dorset Railway Trust, founded in 1966, is the guardian of its records and traditions, and membership is a must for anyone who would study its history or help secure its future. It has a representative collection of equipment, ranging from handlamps and tickets to a complete reconstruction of Midford signalbox, and historic items, from the spade which cut the first sod on the Dorset Central Railway to the last steam locomotive used in the Somerset Coalfield. By force of circumstance it is a government in exile, with its headquarters at Washford station on the West Somerset Railway, but the mere fact of the annexation of its original ground has clearly not wearied this remarkable railway company, determined and independent as it has been throughout its 150 years.

Nowadays anyone can become a participant, and everyone is invited to apply to:

The Somerset & Dorset Railway Trust
'Halcyon', West Road, Bridport,
Dorset DT6 6AA.

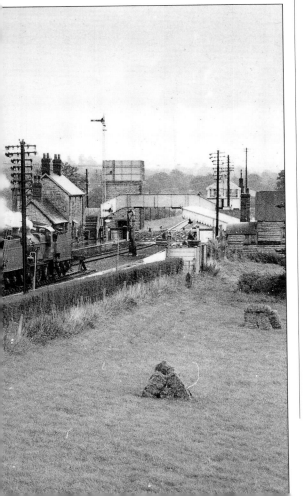

Watering tank engines at Evercreech Junction
Above: 1935. Midland 0-4-4T No 1298 at the south end, probably after arriving from Highbridge. *IAL*

Below: 1965. BR 2-6-4T No 80013 at the north end on 25 October, with a Southern coach. *E. W. J. Crawforth*

Above: A view from an up train departing from Templecombe station after the reversing movement required in order to reach it. This is looking back, and at the rear end is the engine which had hauled the train back into the station. *E. W. J. Crawforth*

Below: Looking forward, the train engine crossing to the up line on the short double-track section down to No 2 Junction. These views were taken on 24 March 1960. *E. W. J. Crawforth*

Above: Locomotive operation consists basically of forcing various intractable substances into, and out of, confined spaces. The crew extracting ash from 2-8-0 No 90 (now No 53810) on the pit at Templecombe pause to watch Bulleid Pacific No 34047 *Callington* pass with the 'Pines Express'; 1 July 1961. *J. C. Haydon*

Below: Freight train banking in the 1930s. A down train emerging from Devonshire Tunnel, which it has filled with steam — the white blob in the background. 2-8-0 No 87 (now No 13807) is hauling 27 wagons, banked by an 0-6-0 facing the other way and pushing tender-first. *Real Photographs*

Above: The classic S&D scene of a down freight passing through Midsomer Norton on a Saturday in early summer. It is the 12.35pm Bath-Evercreech Junction. The train engine is No 86 (now No 53806) and the banker is 0-6-0T No 47496. *R. E. Toop*

Right: An 0-6-0T banking a coal train out of Radstock. The eruption from that engine gives you some idea of the latent power which can be packed into a boiler in the form of steam. *B. A. Butt*

Left: When looking forward, we often wish we could foresee the future but, looking back, we realise that it is as well that we cannot. These men showing off the new Fox, Walker engine No 5 at Radstock in 1875 did not know that within a year she would be in violent head-on collision with No 7 not far away. *Bucknall Collection*

Below: A well-known picture of the unusual accident at Ashcott. On 19 August 1949 0-6-0 No 76 (now No 3260) collided with a train on the level crossing with the Eclipse Peat Co line and fell into the South Drain. This shows the recovery attempt, an engine ready to remove the single coach of the mixed train and a crane, out of sight, supporting the back of the tender. The engine had to be cut up on the spot. (One of the pieces may be seen today in the Somerset & Dorset Railway Trust museum.) *LGRP/Bucknall Collection*

3/10/02 £7.99